MARCO  POLO

BUDAPEST

POLAND

CZECH
REPUBLIC

SLOVAKIA

UKRAINE

Budapest

AUSTRIA

ITALY   HUNGARY

SLOVENIA

ROMANIA

CROATIA

BOSNIA
HERZEG.   SERBIA

MNE
AL KS

www.marco-polo.com

FREE!

THE TOURING APP
shows you the way …
including routes and offline maps!

GET MORE OUT OF YOUR MARCO POLO GUIDE

IT'S AS SIMPLE AS THIS

1 go.marco-polo.com/bud

2 download and discover

GO!

WORKS OFFLINE!

SYMBOLS

INSIDER TIP   Insider Tip

★   Highlight

●●●●   Best of...

☼   Scenic view

♺   Responsible travel: for ecological or fair trade aspects

(*)   Telephone numbers that
are not toll-free

**PRICE CATEGORIES
HOTELS**

Expensive   over 47,000 Ft.

Moderate   31,000–47,000 Ft.

Budget   under 31,000 Ft.

Prices are for a double room
per night including breakfast

**PRICE CATEGORIES
RESTAURANTS**

Expensive   over 5,330 Ft.

Moderate   4,075–5,330 Ft.

Budget   under 4,075 Ft.

Prices are for a main course
and a drink

CONTENTS

DID YOU KNOW?
For bookworms & film buffs
→ p. 22
Time to chill → p. 32
Fit in the City → p. 35
Spotlight on sports→ p. 44
From Moscow with love
→ p. 53
Favourite eateries → p. 60
Local specialities → p. 62
More than a good night's
sleep → p. 86
National holidays → p. 109

MAPS IN THE GUIDEBOOK
(124 A1) Page numbers
and coordinates refer to the
street atlas
(0) Site/address located off
the map
Coordinates are also given for
places that are not marked
on the street atlas
General map of Budapest
and the surrounding area
on p. 138/139

(𝄞 A–B 2–3) refers to the
removable pull-out map

INSIDE FRONT COVER:
The best Highlights

INSIDE BACK COVER:
Metro/tram map

The best MARCO POLO Insider Tips

Our top 15 Insider Tips

INSIDER TIP ▶ Perfect summer treat. All year round

Anjuna makes this dream come true, selling delicious ice pops in a wide variety of flavours, all made from natural ingredients and suitable for vegans → **p. 57**

INSIDER TIP ▶ Cosy accomodation

The *Lavender Circus Hostel* is proof that hostels don't have to be uncomfortable, loud and cramped establishments as their reputation suggests. This one is cosy and lovingly furnished → **p. 86**

INSIDER TIP ▶ Style affair

Experience contemporary Hungarian fashion first hand at the *Monofashion Shop* where young designers showcase their latest creations → **p. 72**

INSIDER TIP ▶ Courtly glamour

More and more new spaces can be admired and appreciated in *Gozsdu Court*, a complex of wonderfully restored apartments in the Jewish Quarter → **p. 47**

INSIDER TIP ▶ Miniature coffee house

Csészényi Kávézó és Pörkölő is an enchanting place, selling homemade cakes and splendid types of blends of coffee. Try their hot chocolate with marshmallows in winter or their large selection of lemonades in summer → **p. 58**

INSIDER TIP ▶ Comic strips

Serious comic fans will love the *International Comic Festival* where visitors can find everything from hand-drawn manga art to graphic novels → **p. 108**

INSIDER TIP ▶ Summer in the city

Stress-free playtime: the small *Károlyi Kert* park is a place of relaxation for children, but also for their parents. It is an oasis in the busy city → **p. 107**

INSIDER TIP ▶ Market stall design

Handcrafted, individual items ranging from unicorn pin badges to creative mobile phone cases are for sale on the *Wamp Design Market,* held open-air in Pest in summer and indoor in Buda in winter → **p. 70**

INSIDERTIP **Retro café**
Anyone charmed by the architecture and design of the former Eastern Bloc will love *Bambi Eszpresszó* where you can enjoy a bit to eat with a coffee, beer or spritzer → **p. 76**

INSIDERTIP **Art en suite**
The boutique hotel *Brody House* offers unique accommodation, combining art and exceptional design in every room; the neighbouring Brody Studios (photo left) also houses a nightclub → **p. 86**

INSIDERTIP **Concerts below deck**
On deck the former Ukrainian stone hauler *A38* you can soak in the Danube scenery while the ship's hull serves as the ultimate music venue → **p. 80**

INSIDERTIP **Authentic Hungarian grub**
Honest, authentic Hungarian food doesn't have to cost the earth for it to taste good. The *Pozsonyi Kisvendéglő* is a great place to try local specialities such as goulash soup, chicken paprikash, etc → **p. 60**

INSIDERTIP **Kitsch glamour**
Humana Vintage Butik sells one-off second-hand fashion ranging from shoulder-padded sequin dresses for ladies to flower-power suits for men. Wacky yet stylish items of clothing! → **p. 71**

INSIDERTIP **Panoramic view**
The view from Budapests highest elevation, the *Elisabeth Tower* on János-hegy, is fantastic. Looking down from the Buda Hills the Danube metropolis is at your feet → **p. 54**

INSIDERTIP **Holocaust Memorial**
A row of shoes lined up along the banks of the Danube between the Chain Bridge and Parliament Building honour the Budapest Jews who were executed near the end of World War II (photo below) → **p. 39**

BEST OF...

FOR FREE

● *Island break*

The 2-km/1.25 mile long, car-free *Margaret Island* is a leisure space that costs nothing. The green spaces are lovely places for picnics, the paths and gardens are perfect for extended walks. Pretty destinations are the water tower, the musical fountain and the Japanese garden → p. 38

● *Pilgrimage à la Ottoman*

Looking to escape the crowds of tourists and avoid paying the entrance ticket to the Fisherman's Bastion? Yet still want to capture the magnificent views over the Danube and Budapest? Then visit the *Tomb of Gül Baba* situated at the foot of the Rózsadomb. It is a popular pilgrimage place for Muslims with its nostalgic Ottoman charm → p. 53

● *Cultural treat on public holidays*

To celebrate their three public holidays, some of Budapest's best museums, including the *Museum of Fine Arts,* offer free admission to everyone on March 15, August 20 and October 23 → p. 44

● *Church in the rock*

The monks ought to charge an entrance fee for this experience: those who take a time out from their sightseeing marathon will find shelter in the *Gellért rock chapel*, an oasis of calm in a small cave, away from all the hustle and bustle (photo) → p. 33

● *Enter the New Year with live music*

The *New Year's Eve* celebrations in Budapest are something very special and for free. There are stages offering live music, often featuring popular Hungarian bands, and traditionally toy-horns are used to make a hell of a noise. Get in a good mood and enjoy the fun → p. 109

● *Shed calories, not forints*

Work out for free at one of Budapest's downtown outdoor gyms which are open to the public. A popular venue, especially amongst joggers, is the *fitness park under the Margaret Bridge* → p. 35

(I I I) Dots in guidebook refer to "Best of..." tips

ONLY IN BUDAPEST
Unique experiences

● *Iconic Bridge*

Spanning across the Danube and weighing several
thousand tons, the iron and stone *Chain Bridge*
is Budapest's vibrant landmark. During the day,
bustling business people and strolling tourists cross from one side to the other while
late in the evening, the bridge is the perfect spot to watch the city fall asleep. A
truly magical experience (photo) → **p. 37**

● *Place to be*

When it comes to lifestyle and nightlife,
Liszt Ferenc tér, also called "Budapest
Broadway", sets the tone. Here, not far from
the elegant boulevard Andrássy út, you will
find one hip café next to another → **p. 44**

● *Incredible ambience*

The *New York Kávéház* is brilliant! You should see this café
at least once, for it is the most breathtaking representative of the
Budapest café tradition: other cafés may be cosier, but here visitors
can feast their eyes on the overwhelming décor → **p. 59**

● *Fairytale castle in the municipal forest*

The fairytale *Vajdahunyad castle* became a public magnet in 1896
when Hungarian patriots celebrated the 1000th anniversary of the
"land conquest" with a great exhibition. The imaginative mix of different architectural styles was aimed at celebrating the achievement of
Hungarian architecture. Today the castle offers a romantic backdrop
for high class summer concerts → **p. 46**

● *Courtyard scene*

The courtyards of the old Jewish quarters between Rákóczi út and Király
utca have turned into the most popular night life locations. In all places where buildings were threatened by decay, alternative "ruin pubs"
have established themselves – for example the *Szimpla kert* → **p. 77**

● *Remembrance and experience*

The Moorish-Byzantine onion domes of the *Dohány Street Synagogue*
are the landmark of an urban cosmos that is unique in Europe: a once
again very lively Jewish Quarter. The synagogue is a very handsome
building, but it's also a memorial to all those who suffered and per-
ished during the times of the ghetto → **p. 49**

ONLY IN

BEST OF...

● *Sunday brunch*
Rainy Sundays are best enjoyed at a slow pace. Head to *Déryné Bisztró* for its ample brunch menu in elegant yet relaxing atmosphere accompanied by live music → p. 61

● *A villa full of art*
At the *Kogart* on the elegant Andrássy út you are surrounded by outstanding works of art. The smart villa houses one of the largest private Hungarian collections of contemporary art → p. 44

● *Welcome to the opera*
The magnificence of the Renaissance revival: just a glance into the foyer will convince you that a guided tour through the *Opera House* is worthwhile → p. 45

● *Delicious fast food*
The *Central Market Hall* sells every conceivable Hungarian culinary delicacy. Don't miss the *lángos* (photo) stall on the first floor: this is the only place to experience just how tasty a stuffed potato-yeast flatbread can be → p. 64

● *Fascinating underwater world*
In the south of Buda, the Campona shopping centre houses the *Tropicarium,* an entertaining, family-friendly aquarium where you can discover some of the ocean's wonders → p. 107

● *Budapest from below*
Budapest is also a city of caves. In the Buda Hills visitors can go down into the *Pálvölgyi cave* and the *Szemlőhegyi cave* and admire the capital from below → p. 53

RAIN

RELAX AND CHILL OUT
Take it easy and spoil yourself

● *Bathing in beer*
Tired of sightseeing? Then treat yourself to a pampering session at the *Beer Spa*. Relax in their cosy wooden bath tubs filled with a mixture of bubbly mineral water and natural beer ingredients. And of course the liquid gold is also available to drink! → **p. 32**

● *Cruising on the Danube*
The beauty of the Hungarian capital is seen in its full glory from the river. Relax and enjoy the impressive panorama on a *boat tour on the Danube* – with a pleasant breeze on a summer evening (photo) → **p. 32**

● *Chilling out on the bridge*
A popular meeting spot for young people in Budapest is *Liberty Bridge,* provided the weather is fine. Sitting on its green metal construction, you are treated to delightful views of the Danube while enjoying a glass of beer or lemonade → **p. 50**

● *Sounds for the soul*
The *Budapest Klezmer Band* is a leading exponent of a kind of music that is conquering ever larger audiences, be it in clubs or at the annual Jewish Art Days Festival. The rousing mix of melancholy and jolly sounds is a wonderful treat for the soul → **p. 108**

● *Bathing pleasures*
The *Széchenyi Baths* in the municipal forest is an architectural oasis of luxury. With their warm water the open-air thermal pools are a pleasure in any weather → **p. 45**

● *Classical sounds*
The *Béla Bartók Concert Hall* is part of the Palace of Arts. This hi-tech hall has excellent acoustics. Come here to enjoy concerts by the Hungarian National Philharmonic Orchestra and performances by orchestras and soloists from around the world → **p. 78**

INTRODUCTION

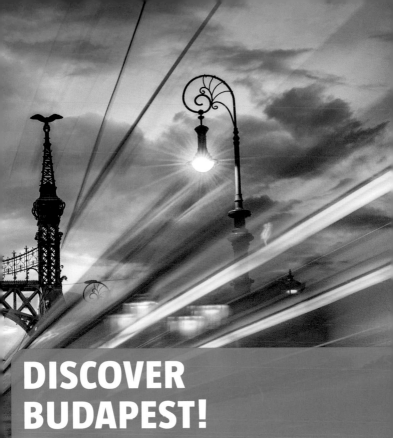

DISCOVER BUDAPEST!

You can twist it and turn it as much as you like but the city of Budapest - whether viewed from above, below, or from the Danube water - is always spectacular, warts and all. Admittedly, the city has its blemishes: the crumbling plaster on its hundreds of year-old buildings, its questionable politics played out in Parliament, the obstinate inhabitants with their deeply rooted melancholy. Once bitten, you will struggle to shake off *Budapest's enticing charm:* The view of Budapest lit up at night from the Fisherman's Bastion is just as hypnotizing as a ride on a tram through the city by day with *views of the Danube* across the Liberty Bridge. For many visitors it is love at first sight.

The city's lovable appeal undoubtedly lies in its imperfections, the *absurd contrasts.* The most predominant of which are Buda and Pest, the two juxtaposing halves of the city, split by the Danube River yet united by their charm. Discover for yourself how the two sides differ in terms of their ambience, architecture and history. Yet what's certain is that the heights of the green Buda Hills and the *retro urban flair* of the upper class townhouses in Pest belong together like two peas in a pod.

Photo: Liberty Bridge

Even a good 25 years after the fall of Communism in Hungary, Budapest is still a city in the midst of change and upheaval. It is striving for authenticity, modernity and a higher quality of life. The city looks more glamorous every year. One example of this urban development is the **"New City Centre project",** a traffic-free zone which spreads from Szabadság tér, Liberty Square, south to Kálvin tér. The central squares, including Kossuth Lajos tér in front of the Parliament building, have been renovated and the Redoute in Pest along the banks of the Danube has been restored to its former charm. This also applies to the magnificent Liszt-Ferenc Music Academy on Liszt Ferenc tér.

> **The city's lovable appeal undoubtedly lies in its imperfections**

The next large-scale building project on the city's agenda is **"Liget Budapest"**: The city's woodland behind Heroes' Square is to be redesigned by 2020 and new or contemporary cultural institutions such as the House of Hungarian Music and the Transport Museum are to be brought to life again. Budapest locals remain sceptical: building projects in Hungary are increasingly tainted by corruption while hospitals and schools in the city and countryside are left to corrode. And anyway, Hungarians seek refuge in old *traditions*. Although denouncing their country's socialist past, they also harbour a nostalgic affection for these former times.

The view from the Fisherman's Bastion to the Parliament is simply breathtaking

Known colloquially as the *"Heart of Europe"* or *"Queen of the Danube"*, the capital is home to around 1.7 million people. Its population speaks volumes about the city's significance when you consider than the entire population of Hungary is 9.8 million. Many Hungarians relocate from the province to the big city to study or in search of work and better living conditions – or further afield to Germany or Austria, seduced by the Euro. The demographic trend over the past years shows that increasingly more Hungarians, especially singles under 40, are leaving their home towns to *work abroad*. Some of them return due to homesickness. Take Ági for example: Born in Budapest, this 26-year old works, as many Hungarians her age, for a multinational organisation as a team leader and earns net 300,000 forints, a well above-average wage by Hungarian standards. With the help of a bank loan and her own savings, she has recently joined the property ladder as a first-time buyer and can finally stop paying the soaring rents in the capital.

Budapest has the highest wages in the country. Yet it is almost impossible for

> **In the summer, Budapest is one open air eldorado**

most people to get rich from working. The cost of living is as high as in Western countries; as a result wages only allow for a modest existence. Everyday life is tough for most people in Budapest. Nevertheless they are *their city's biggest fans.* That is because Budapest is where the action is: international music stars only perform in the capital and it is only here that major sporting events and festivals are held. The city is also the best departure point for travelling.

During the summer months Budapest is a veritable *open-air Mecca*. The banks of the Danube and Margaret Island, the municipal forest and the parks are all places the people of Budapest like to flock to every free minute they get. They go outside – and they go out. That is also true of families: Szilvi and Tomi and their two children live in one of the prefab high-rise apartment blocks on the Buda side of the city. They have a tight budget, but there's no penny-pinching when it comes to *quality time* with their children. Their pride and joy is their own car – a red Suzuki Swift, one of the most popular cars in Hungary. The zoo, the children's railway, rollerblading on Margaret Island, trips to the Buda Hills are all things this family enjoys, making Budapest a colourful place for them to live in. Join them, and pack your rollerblades, too!

Márta is a representative of the older generation: she was born in Budapest and has remained loyal to the city her whole life. You can meet the pensioner in a *coffee house*. Chatting with her friends there with a piece of *Dobos-torta* is a must, she says, even though her monthly pension of 80,000 forints is not really enough to justify it. Among her other pleasures are visits to the *thermal baths*. Budapest's thermal baths are more than just spas, especially for the older people; they are places to enjoy and to meet people. A trip to Budapest would not be complete without these two: a visit to the traditional coffee houses and thermal baths.

The people of Budapest are well practised in making the best of things. And there is one thing in particular that they all have in common: they are **proud to be from the capital**, blessed with the unshakable self-confidence that comes from knowing that they set the pace and the tone. They may spend the week in the city, but during the summer months at least, the exodus begins on Fridays. The most popular **destinations** are the nearby Lake Velence, Lake Balaton and the Danube Bend. Among the people who like to escape the city will be those who managed to acquire a little holiday getaway during the country's Communist years, or those visiting friends and relatives. Alternatively, they may be travelling with holiday vouchers, a form of holiday pay issued by companies. The people of Budapest are city people of a somewhat different, typically Hungarian kind. The "we" is more important than the "I", and **family ties** are hugely important. Family members stick together, celebrate birthdays, Easter and Christmas together and are the most important source of support in times of need. Social relationships define everyday life at every age: students find **friends for life** in their halls of residence; they celebrate and cook together. Expensive cinema and nightclub visits are the exception, but they still know how to have lots of fun.

> **On the feast of St Stephen, people celebrate on streets and squares**

On the **Feast of St Stephen** of Hungary, the most important national holiday, celebrated on 20 August, hundreds of thousands of people from Budapest take to the streets, squares and bridges. History is omnipresent in the minds of everyone in Budapest. It all began in 896 with the "land seizure" of the seven Magyar tribes under the leadership of Grand Prince Árpád. The **first king of Hungary**, Stephen I, whose coronation took place in AD 1000, is especially revered. The Crown of St Stephen is on display in the Hungarian Parliament Building in Budapest. After the Mongols overran the country in 1241–2, Béla IV of Hungary built the first fortress on Castle Hill. Matthias Corvinus, King of Hungary from 1458–90, had it extended in the Renaissance style. This Golden Age was followed by 160 years of continuous occupation by the Turks (1526–1668). By the time the battle against the occupying power was successfully won, Buda and Pest were completely destroyed.

In 1941, Hungary took Germany's side in World War II against the Soviet Union. During the Nazi reign of terror, supported by the Hungarian Arrow Cross Party, Budapest's **Jewish Quarter** was turned into a ghetto and a graveyard for thousands. At the end of the war large areas of the city lay in ruins. In 1947 the Communist Party came to power. Protests by students in Budapest triggered resistance against the regime in 1956, but the revolt of the "counter-revolutionaries" was brutally suppressed. Decades later in the night leading up to 11 September 1989, Hungary opened its borders, allowing around 100,000 East German citizens, including many who had been put up in a camp in Budapest, to escape. On 23 October, on the 33rd anniversary of the Revolution of 1956, the **Republic of Hungary** was proclaimed from a window of the Hungarian Parliament Building. That marked the end of the Communist People's Republic.

For the past 25 years, the spotlight in Budapest has been focused mainly on the *flourishing cityscapes*: the wonderfully restored beacons of historic Budapest, the huge international investments in shopping centres and luxury real estate, and on large projects such as the Millennium Quarter around Rákóczi Bridge. The *darker sides of progress* have tended to be ignored, however. The most recent economic crisis has increased public-sector financial problems as well as social tensions. Even in liberal Budapest, the word "international" does not have a good ring to it anymore. On the one hand, international corporations based in the capital are important investors and employers yet, on the other hand, they also represent the banks to whom many homeowners are in debt and are at risk of losing the roof over their head. As *the country's political and economic centre*, Budapest is a kind of lens that concentrates all these problems.

21st century temple of art: National Theatre in the Millennium District on the Pest Danube banks

People are taking stock in the capital. The most important question is: in what way have the past 25 years benefited "ordinary" Hungarians? Budapest is focusing more than ever on the difficult living conditions of the majority and on the city's unique Hungarian identity. The people of the city want the Budapest of tomorrow to be different. What should it look like? The answer is not yet clear. The *beauty of the city* remains untouched by all of that. It seeps its way through the cracks in the crumbling house walls and in the burning hot asphalt. It radiates from the *magical courtyards in Pest* and the refurbished metro stations as well as from the gestures of the humorous Hungarians. Are you smitten?

Magical courtyards and charming gestures

WHAT'S HOT

1 Get moving

Modern dance Acrobatics, performance, experimental theatre and installation – the offline:ontheater dance group *(www.offlineon.eu)* perform reinterpretations of contemporary dance. *Trafó (Liliom utca 41 | www.trafo.hu) (photo)* is a platform for artistic innovation and experimentation where both Hungarian and international dancers perform. Definitely worth a visit is the international festival for modern dance *Szóló Duó (www.szoloduo.com)* held every year at *MU Színház (Kőrösy József utca 17 | www.mu.hu)*.

2 Re-design

Original new uses It doesn't always have to be brand new! Many items and material ranging from textiles and PVC to paper can often be creatively upcycled. You can find glasses made of old vinyl and film reels at *Tipton Eyeworks (Belgrád rakpart 26 | www.vinylize.com)(photo)*, while *Karton Design (Szent István utca 102 | Törökbálint | www.kartondesign.com)* just outside the city produces furniture from cardboard.

3 Decorative

Individual and handmade The people of Budapest love wearing unusual accessories. Very popular are the jewellery artworks by goldsmith *Márta Edőcs (www.martaedocs.hu)* and the unusual designs by *Fanni Király (www.kiralyfanni.com) (photo)*. *Regina Kaintz (www.reginakaintz.com)* often uses barbed wire in her pieces, in combination with gemstones. The leading showcase for small-scale jewellery designers is *Magma* gallery *(Petőfi Sándor utca 11 | www.magma.hu)*.

Vegetarian heaven

Meatless goulash Vegan restaurants keep popping up like mushrooms all over Budapest. The city also offers a great selection of meat-free street food, for example the *Las Vegan's food trucks (VII | Street Food Karavan | Kazinczy utca 18; XI | promenade next to the Allee shopping centre)*, at *Istvánffi Veggie Burger (V | Királyi Pál utca 20; III | Lajos utca 36)* or *Vegan Love (XI | Bartók Béla út 9 | www.veganlove.hu)*. If you prefer Hungarian-Near East fusion cuisine, then head to the food truck belonging to Hungary's most famous vegan blogger, Kristóf Steiner *(Kristóf Konyhája in the Food Truck Garden | IX | Üllői út 51)*. Despite the wide choice of vegetarian food available, don't expect that everyone knows what vegan means – Hungary's older generation especially don't regard "a little bit of chicken or fish" as carnivorous food...

4

Puzzle rooms

5

Let me out of here! The concept of escape or exit games was invented in Hungary's capital which is why the rooms are real crowd-pullers. The original Budapest adventure games are also far more inventive and creative than the copy-cat rooms abroad. *E-Exit (Nyár utca 27 | www.szabadulos-jatek.hu)* has four rooms, including an exciting George Orwell inspired "1984" escape room. *Claustrophilia (Erzsébet körút 8 | www.claustrophilia.hu)* is smaller in size yet the rooms change themes twice a year and the puzzles are always very tricky. The thrilling exit games in *Moviescape (Bajcsy Zsilinszky köz 2 | www.moviescape.hu)* are based on films such as "The Ring" and Tim Burton's "Alice in Wonderland".

IN A NUTSHELL

BUDA OR PEST?

Although the people from Budapest are extremely proud of their magnificent city, local patriotism is not widely spread in the capital. It matters little to locals whether someone was born in Budapest or has moved here from the countryside. A far more telling fact, however, is on which bank of the Danube a Budapest local lives. Despite the official unification of Óbuda and Pest in 1873, the 'Buda vs. Pest' debate is still as heated today as ever before and locals are unable to agree on which side of the city is better. Built on a series of green hills, Buda is the calmer and prettier side yet Pest locals would say Buda inhabitants are snobbish, old and boring – well that's the cliché anyway. In contrast, Pest is the party and nightlife district and too loud, dirty and shabby for many Buda citizens who only cross the river to work and go out in the evenings. Of course, there are distinctive characteristics to both sides yet this unlikely pair can only be fully appreciated when seen as a united city. So take a stroll on a sunny day over the Margaret Bridge, enjoy the view of both banks of the Danube and listen to Róbert Rátonyis' love song "Budapest, Budapest, te csodás!" (Budapest, you are wonderful). Reconciliation guaranteed!!

INVENTIVE FOLK

What do the ballpoint pen (biro), Rubik's Cube *(Rubik-kocka)* and Vitamin C have in common? They were all invented

More than just tradition: Budapest stands for the Danube and thermal baths, and for a country undergoing radical economic change

or discovered by Hungarians. It's a fact and the Magyars are extremely proud of their inventive spirit. They are only too happy to tell visitors about the momentous inventions which started life in their small country. Today, this spirit of innovation lives on in young Hungarian start-up companies, some of which have achieved international acclaim. For example, Prezi, the digital presentation tool developed in 2007 by the artist Ádám Somlai-Fischer and IT programmer Péter Halácsy; just two years after its founding, Prezi was opened in U.S Silicon Valley and is today used all over the world.

HIDDEN GEMS

Admittedly, the buildings are beautiful from the outside, but it's what's inside that really counts. Budapest is namely full of courtyards and "ruin pubs and bars", which are worth visiting. The courtyards often belong to former bourgeois houses in Pest or desolated industrial buildings which have been transformed into chic restaurants, pubs, clubs or hotels by entrepreneurial restaurateurs. Formerly the Haggenmacher Palace (Haggenmacher-palota) built in 1886, the *Andrássy út 52* is now a multi-purpose venue, functioning as the Ervin-Szabó library by day and the trendy *Hello Baby Bar* by night. Although the ravages of time have left their mark on the peristyle, arcades and tiles, this patina only adds to the building's charm. With its splendid paved mosaic floor and plant-covered facades, the courtyard of the 1877-built Almássy Palace (Almássy-palota) *(Ötpacsirta utca 2)* is, in contrast, an oasis in the middle of the city housing the recommended restaurant *Építészpince.* And if you visit the confectionery Auguszt (see p. 58) make sure to take a peek in the courtyard which is now home to *Paloma,* a co-working showroom for artists and designers.

UNDERGROUND WORLD

Can you imagine a room in which 350 double-decker buses would fit side by side? No, not an aircraft hangar but a gigantic, underwater labyrinth of caves right underneath the Buda side of Budapest. The city's historic thermal baths derive their heat from these hot thermal springs deep beneath the capital. Budapest is home to the largest collection of thermal caves in the world. Divers with a cave diving certification can take part, for example, in a guided diving session in warm waters of 21–27 degrees. But you don't have to get wet to visit other caves: In district II, the stalactites and mineral formations in the Pálvölgyi and Szemlohegyi caves can be admired on dry land. There are even cave areas suitable for sufferers of claustrophobia: the Hospital in the Rock in the Castle district and the Gellért Rock Chapel.

FOR BOOKWORMS & FILM BUFFS

The Monster – (2013) You don't need to have read "The Only Man on the Continent" to be hooked by this sequel novel. Terézia Mora was awarded the German Book Prize for her book about melancholy, grief and death.

Sátántangó – (2011) Set in a remote village in rural Hungary, this novel by László Krasznahorkai captures the isolation of its residents and the despair of rural Hungary in the Communist era. An extremely popular writer in the English-speaking world!

For some inexplicable reason – (2014) This feature film by director Gábor Reisz is about the film student Áron which is funny, honest and very Hungarian in style. The film is recommended to get you in the mood for your trip to Budapest and when you're there you can follow in Áron's footsteps to the bar, street and the HÉV tram stop which all appear in the film.

Son of Saul – Set in the Auschwitz concentration camp in October 1944, the film follows two days in the life of Saul Ausländer, a Hungarian Jew, who works there. This holocaust drama is the work of director László Nemes Jeles who won an Oscar for the film in 2016 in the "Best Foreign Language Film" category.

THE POETRY OF COFFEE HOUSES

Cigarette smoke, heated discussions and the noise of turning newspapers: Budapest coffee houses were intellectual hotspots for writers, journalists and artists at the end of the 19th and beginning of the 20th century. Opened in 1894, the legendary New York café even offered the poor writers free paper and ink and access to the "writer's bowl" at a small expense. Today there is little left of the authentic atmosphere yet the magnificent interior, first-class service and amazing desserts, such as the *Dobos-torta,* more than compensate.

RIVER ENCOUNTERS

The Danube River is both so near and yet so far in Budapest. Although it connects the two halves, Buda and Pest, stones and other barriers separate man from water almost everywhere in the capital. The best way to get closer to the river is on a bike tour or by HÉV along the northern bank to the Rómaipart (Roman banks) in the north of Buda and let your feet dangle in the water at the open-air bar *Fellini.* At the annual dragon boat festival held in May on the peninsula Kopaszi gát, you can watch as others take to the water. The Danube is also the secret star on 20 August, Saint Stephan's National Holiday, when the bombastic firework display is reflected in its waters.

Sweet delicacies at the Gerbeaud coffee house

QUICK TONGUES

In Hungarian, the word for "quick-witted" is *talpraesett* and literally translates as "fallen on your feet"- not in terms of luck but of humour. The people of the city always have a joke at hand and an opinion on everything whether they understand it or not. One witty example of Hungarian humour is the TV journalist Olga Kálmán who invites guests from all political spectrums to take part in her political talk show. When a politician presented her with a bottle of perfume as a gift before the show, she retorted, "Well I'd have preferred a watering can for the garden"!

UNDER ORBÁN'S IRON THUMB

Right-wing extremism, dictatorship, Eurosceptic — these are just some of the less-flattering headlines used by the international press to describe Hungary under Viktor Orbán. Many locals have also now had enough of "Orbánistan" which has been responsible for many absurd changes in the legislation, corruption scandals and no real improvements to living standards. Poverty has been on the increase for years and the social gap is widening. Tens of thousands of protesters marched through Budapest to take part in demonstrations against a planned internet tax or an anti-foreign law imposing strict restrictions on NGOs that receive foreign funding. Despite this discontentment, the right-wing national Fidesz, Orbán's political party, continues to enjoy popularity in the political polls. The second largest party is the extreme-right Jobbik party, which has radical and xenophobic roots, despite its moderate appearance. But there is reason for hope and optimism: Momentum was founded in 2016 by a group of young intellectuals who caused a stir for starting off a petition against the Budapest bid for the 2024 Summer Olympics. The reason for the petition was that many Hungarians want good hospitals and schools rather than international sporting events. And Orbán has yet to deliver his promises.

ART NOUVEAU À LA BUDAPEST

The industrial boom starting in 1870 had a noticeable effect on Budapest's architecture and led to Hungary's own interpretation of Art Nouveau which flourished at the turn of the century. Hungarian Art Nouveau is characterised by ornate but not tacky decadence with its own unique architecture influenced by international styles. It is no coincidence that the leading figure of Hungarian Art Nouveau Ödön Lechner (1845–1914) is often referred to as the "Hungarian Gaudi" after the Catalan star architect, Antoni Gaudí. The best way to admire the many examples of Art Nouveau architecture is to take a tour of the city: Several masterpieces can be found on the edge of the city's municipal forest, e.g. the Egger Villa *(Városligeti fasor 24)*. A secret gem is

Swim like a king: the Széchenyi Bath looks like a palace

the large-scale building belonging to the Institute for Geography and Geophysics (Magyar Földtani és Geofizikai Intézet) *(Stefánia út 14)*, designed by Lechner himself. The building is roofed with amazing sky-blue Zsolnay ceramic tiles and a gigantic globe supported by four figures. Both the inside and outside are adorned with spectacular folkloric decorative elements. It seems laughable that Franz Joseph I of Austria, on a state visit to Budapest, dared to utter his dissatisfaction with the building's exterior!

THE STIGMA ATTACHED TO THE ROMANI PEOPLE

Commonly known by the exonym gypsies, the Roma are an itinerant ethnic group often characterised by their colourful head scarves, gold jewellery and fiddle under their arms. Originating from the Pannonian Basin in Central Europe, most of the Roma in Budapest have lived here for centuries and are no less Hungarian than their neighbours, yet they are still treated as outsiders. Every taxi driver can tell you prejudiced "truths" about the *cigányok* (gypsies) and will quickly warn you against visiting districts inhabited by the Roma. In fact, a significant proportion of the Hungarian population is made up of approx. 600,000–800,000 Roma. For many, music is an escape from this poverty and discrimination – especially because the Roma musicians have traditionally been held in high esteem in Hungary. This tradition inspired the jazz guitarist Ferenc Snétberger to establish a centre for talented musicians *(www.snetbergercenter.org)* which regularly organises concerts for young Roma people. The cultural centres *Auróra* and *Gólya* in district VIII also work hard to promote dialogue between the minority and majority.

ECCENTRIC LANGUAGE

Megszentségteleníthetetlenségeskedéseitekért – no, not a typing error, with 44 letters is officially the longest word in the Hungarian language. It means something like "for your continued behaviour as if you could not be desecrated". It is almost never used but is still a good example of the complexity of the Hungarian language. Contrary to common belief, Hungarian does not belong to the Slavic but the Finno-Ugric family of languages. Hungarian, like most other languages, has started to borrow at an accelerated rate English words over the last few decades. Examples include mobil, szponzor, szuper, sport and muffin.

WARM WATER SPRINGS

Budapest sits on a labyrinth of thermal springs and a bathing tradition which stretches back to Roman times. Although they lack the cleanliness and hygiene of spic-and-span modern spas, the baths stand as a legacy of former times; the Király Bath may look a little rough around the edges but it actually dates back to the Ottoman period. And despite the rotten egg odour of the sulphur water basin at the Rudas Bath, you can still have a great deal of fun in these natural healing waters. The outdoor pool at the Széchenyi Baths is fantastic in winter when a thick misty fog develops above the water caused by the cold outside temperatures. Or simply go to the Gellért Baths to watch the dignified old men and women in their bathing caps swimming their lengths.

SIGHTSEEING

CITY **WHERE TO START?**
Vörösmarty tér (124 C2)
(🗺 D9): Vörösmarty Square in Pest is an ideal starting point for exploring the city. The elegant white building on the front side houses the legendary Café Gerbeaud. A highlight to the north of the square is St Stephen's Basilica, while the shopping street Váci utca can be found to the south. The panorama from the nearby Vigadó tér/Danube Embankment is stunning: the views across the river extend from Gellért Hill along Castle Hill all the way to the Chain Bridge. Vörösmarty tér is served by metro line 1 *(Földalatti)*.

"I am from San Francisco, and San Francisco is the most beautiful city, but Budapest isn't far behind with that." – was Tom Hanks' verdict when he came to the Hungarian capital in 2015 to shoot the film "Inferno".

But guess what? The Hollywood actor is wrong: Budapest is in fact the nicer of the two cities. The only problem being you are spoilt for choice as to what you visit first. Do you start back in medieval times at the Castle in Buda? In sacral Neo-Renaissance at Saint Stephen's Basilica in Pest? Or in modern times with contemporary architecture in the shape of a great glass whale, the *Bálna?* Or do you just follow your appetite and go for a large, deep-fried *lángos* topped with soured cream and cheese? Don't pan-

Churches, synagogues and palaces: the enormous diversity of architectural styles in Budapest has become a style in itself

Ic: whatever you decide, you'll have enough time to pack in all the sights even if you're only staying in Budapest for a long weekend. The city was made to be explored on foot. And don't forget to look up sometimes: although they appear decaying and crumbling at first glance, the city's buildings all have tales to tell, featuring ornamental Art Nouveau details and amusing, pathetic statues or a cheesy retro store sign and even the odd cat staring down at you from a balcony above.

All in all, Budapest is an eclectic mix of ruggedness and unshaven charm. One moment you are firmly in the city's past enjoying a sweet slice of *dobos-torta* in a coffee house – while the next you are abruptly confronted by the city's present with the sad sight of many homeless people living on the streets. Budapest has recently clamped down on homelessness and declared the area around all UNESCO heritage sites (e.g., in the Castle Quarter) a homeless-free zone. However, you can still help the city's homeless

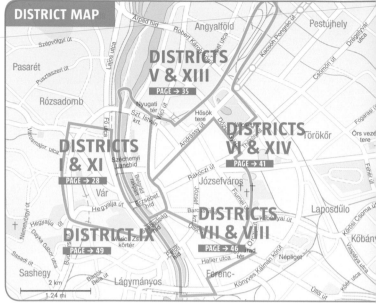

DISTRICT MAP

Szépvölgyi út

Pasarét

Rózsadomb

Árpád híd

Róbert Károly

Angyalföld

Pestújhely

DISTRICTS V & XIII

PAGE → 35

DISTRICTS I & XI

PAGE → 28

Vár

DISTRICTS VI & XIV

PAGE → 41

DISTRICTS VII & VIII

PAGE → 46

DISTRICT IX

PAGE → 49

Sashegy

2 km

1.24 mi

Lágymányos

Ferenc-

The map shows the location of the most interesting districts. There is a detailed map of each district on which each of the sights described is numbered.

population by purchasing the Hungarian equivalent of The Big Issue called "FN" *(Fedél nélkül,* "without a cover"). You decide how much you want to donate, the recommended minimum is 100 forints – the homeless sellers get to keep all their takings.

DISTRICTS I & XI

Districts I (Budavár/Buda Castle) and XI (Újbuda/New Buda) are situated on the western bank of the Danube and they also include parts of the Buda Hills in the hinterland, one of the city's preferred residential and recreational areas. Visitors particularly enjoy exploring

the sites close to the Danube, first and foremost the Castle Quarter. Of District I's 25,000 inhabitants, 2,500 still live in the alleys of the Castle Quarter. The Castle Hill ensemble is a fascinating mix. You will find parts of the Baroque town from the 17th century, traces of the medieval town and a lot of showy architecture from the 19th century. Towards the Danube, the most impressive area is between Buda Castle and Matthias Church. The underground world of Castle Hill is also quite striking. A vast system of passageways extends deep into the hill for several kilometres.

The Castle Quarter's southern neighbour is Gellért Hill in District XI (population: 140,000) with the Citadel and the imposing Liberty Statue. As is demonstrated by its highly symbolic monuments, not to mention the outstanding architecture of the Gellért Hotel (once the city's most sought-after grand hotel), the section of District XI close to the city centre is one of the grandest parts of Budapest, and the posh villas on Gellért Hill still make it one of the city's most expensive residential areas.

■1■ CASTLE GARDEN BAZAAR (VÁR-KERT BAZÁR) (127 E5–6) (*ØØ C10*)

Are you fed up following the crowds, dashing from one attraction to the next and would prefer to simply hang out for a while? Then head to the Castle Garden Bazaar on the banks of the Danube beneath the castle. If the word bazaar conjures up images of the bustling markets in Istanbul, you are not too far from the truth - in as far as the past is concerned. Following the bazaar's completion in 1883, the site was not only a busy trading place, the building complex with gardens also housed artists' studios. The bazaar was designed by Miklós Ybl, one of the most talented Hungarian architects of his time, and completely renovated from 2011 to 2014. The garden and open-air area is open from 6am to 12 midnight and is particularly enchanting in the evenings when INSIDER TIP lit up enchantingly; exhibitions and concerts are also held in the gardens. Stairs (and lifts for those in a rush) lead you up to Castle Hill. *I | Ybl Miklós tér | www.varkertbazar.hu | tram 19, 41 Clark Ádám tér | bus 16, 105*

■2■ BUDA CASTLE (BUDAVÁRI PALOTA) ★ ⬣ (127 D–E5) (*ØØ B9–10*)

There's a lot to discover up here. First and foremost, the spectacular view over Budapest and the Danube as it weaves its way through the city and under the bridges which connect the city's two halves. The city's history is also depicted by the beautifully decorative statues dotted around the gardens. What else can we say...oh yes, the Castle Palace is Hungary's largest building and it's easy to lose your way around here – as do many a Budapest local. But don't worry you can't get irrevocably lost: the entire castle district is just 1.5 km/1 mile long. Buda Castle, the city's monumental landmark, was destroyed three times between the 13th and 20th centuries, but always rebuilt in the style of the particular era – originally with Gothic elements, later with Renaissance and Baroque ones. An interesting mixture! Buda Castle now houses the Hungarian National Gallery, the History Museum and the National Széchenyi Library. Until the reconstruction work has finished

Castle Hill by night – an illuminating experience

on the Museum of Fine Arts, around 50 works of art from its collection are on exhibition in Building C. While you are up here, keep a lookout for the monstrous bird known as the Turul! This mythological creature dug its claws into a sword on the edge of the Szent György tér in front of the Castle Palace and is today a national symbol for Hungary. *I / Szent György tér | funicular from Clark Ádám tér | bus 16, 105*

▐3▌ HOSPITAL IN THE ROCK (SZIKLAKÓRHÁZ) (126 C3) (*ⅅ B9*)

This place provides an intriguing glimpse of Budapest's underground world and of recent Hungarian history. You will learn all about what was long a state secret known only by the code name *LOSK 0101/1*: a military hospital with an operating theatre and the government's nuclear bunker. The caves were used during World War II by the Nazis, and during the Hungarian Revolution of 1956. The nuclear bunker, which was kept in constant operation, is a relic of the Cold War. *Daily 10am–8pm (hourly guided tours, approx. 60 min.) | I | Lovas út 4c | www.sziklakorhaz.hu | bus 16, 16A, 116*

▐4▌ FISHERMAN'S BASTION (HALÁSZBÁSTYA) ★ ☼ (126 C2–3) (*ⅅ B8*)

You could spend hours up here, mesmerized by the city's stunning panorama and the grandiose Neo-Romanesque architecture of the Fisherman's Bastion. The viewing platforms, towers, walkways and archways all in white-grey stone belong to a fairytale castle and were designed by the architect Frigyes Schulek and built between 1895 and 1902. Don't come here expecting to see fish though – the name is a reminder of the fact that there were once defensive walls here that were secured and defended by the guild of fishermen. *Always accessible | free admission in the evening, at night as well as approx. mid-Oct–mid March and all day on 20 Aug | I | Szentháromság tér | bus 16, 16A, 116*

SIGHTSEEING IN DISTRICTS I & XI

1 Castle Garden Bazaar (Várkert Bazár)

2 Buda Castle (Budavári palota)

3 Hospital in the Rock (Sziklakórház)

4 Fisherman's Bastion (Halászbástya)

5 Liberty Statue (Szabadság szobor)

6 Gellért Baths (Gellért fürdő)

7 Gellért Hill and Citadel (Gellérthegy/Citadella)

8 Gellért Monument (Szt. Gellért szobor)

9 Gellért Rock Chapel (Gellért sziklakápolna)

///// Pedestrian zone

10 Matthias Church (Mátyás templom)

11 Rudas Thermal Baths (Rudas fürdő)

12 Hungarian National Gallery (Magyar Nemzeti Galéria)

5 LIBERTY STATUE (SZABADSÁG SZOBOR) ☆ (124 C5) (*ш C11*)

Although branded by some locals as "bottle opener," Zsigmond Strobl's 14 m/46 ft high statue of a lady with the palm frond proclaiming freedom is a special landmark. Some of her fame is attributed to the local legend surrounding her figure; namely that Miklós Horthy, Hungarian governor from 1920 to 1944, wanted her originally to carry a propeller blade in memory of his son who died in a plane accident during the war. Another reason for the lady's popularity is the amazing view over Budapest, the Danube and its bridges from the foot of this bronze statue erected in 1947. *XI | Citadella sétány | bus 27 or on foot from Szent Gellért tér*

6 GELLÉRT BATHS (GELLÉRT FÜRDŐ) (124 C6) (*ш D11–12*)

A bathhouse looking like straight out of a Wes Anderson film. The decorative Art Nouveau style welcomes guests in the entrance area and the inside walls are covered in magnificent mosaics. The bath is a popular retreat for old Hungarian men and women and (especially) tourists. The outdoor wave pool was a sensation when it was built in these thermal baths almost 100 years ago. *Daily 6am-8pm | XI | Kelenhegyi út 4 | near Hotel Gellért | www.gellertbath.hu | metro 4 Szent Gellért tér | tram 19, 41, 47, 48, 49, 56*

7 GELLÉRT HILL AND CITADEL (GELLÉRTHEGY/CITADELLA) ☆ (124 B–C 5–6) (*ш C11*)

In addition to Castle Hill, the appearance of Buda is also shaped by Gellért Hill, a 130-m/426 ft dolomite colossus. In the mid-19th century the Habsburgs built a citadel on the top of the hill. There are wonderful panoramic views of Castle Hill, the city and the Danube from here. *XI | Citadella sétány | bus 27 or on foot from Szent Gellért tér*

8 GELLÉRT MONUMENT (SZT. GELLÉRT SZOBOR) (124 B4) (*ш C11*)

The statue can be found close to Elisabeth Bridge on Gellért Hill. It commemorates St Gellért (Gerard), who came from Venice in around 1000 AD at the request of King Stephen in order to drive

TIME TO CHILL

Beer and spa in one? Yes you heard correctly; the ● *Beer Spa (daily 10am–7pm | XIV | Állatkerti körút 9–11 | tel. 30 5 15 07 02 | www.thermalbeerspa.com | tram 1)* offers guests the chance to relax in wooden tubs filled with water heated to 36 degrees and a mixture of malt, hops and yeast. Rich in vitamin C, this blend is supposed to do wonders for your skin. You can, of course, enjoy a beer and some Hungarian snacks while you bathe. *Egészségére!* – Cheers! One of the best views of Budapest to which you should absolutely treat yourself is from the water, namely by taking a ● *boat trip on the Danube. Legenda (tel. 1 2 66 41 90 | www.legenda.hu)* is the most popular and professional of the operators. There are different routes and types of trips to choose from – by day or by night with or without candlelight dinner – and with explanations of the sightseeing attractions in English.

forward his programme of Christianisation. Gerard is said to have been nailed to a barrel by heathen Hungarians and hurled down the hill into the Danube.

Daily 8am–8pm | XI | Szent Gellért rakpart | way up near Gellért Baths) | metro 4 Szent Gellért tér | tram 19, 41, 47, 48, 49, 56

700 years old and picture-perfect: the Matthias Church is a fairytale dream

His statue is enclosed by a semi-circular colonnade. *XI | Gellérthegy | bus 7, 107 | tram 18, 19, 41*

9 INSIDER TIP GELLÉRT ROCK CHAPEL (GELLÉRT SZIKLA-KÁPOLNA) ● (124 C6) (*D11*)

The chapel occupies a natural grotto in the side of Gellért Hill. On your way up you can enjoy views of the Danube. Once inside you will find an oasis of tranquility. The church is part of the Paulite monastery that was re-founded in 1989 and is located next door. The four monks enjoy having visitors, and request participation or silence during the services (8:30am, 5pm and 8pm, Sun also 11am).

10 MATTHIAS CHURCH (MÁTYÁS TEMPLOM) (126 C2) (*B8*)

"Like in a fairytale", you may think on seeing the Matthias Church for the first time. Even the square in front – the Szentháromság tér (Trinity Square) – is so enchanting that you may find it hard to pack your camera away. And then there is the church itself – a gem of Neo-Gothic architecture. It is named after King Matthias Corvinus, who still bears the epithet "the just" today and who celebrated both of his weddings here with great pomp. During the Turkish occupation it was used as a mosque, but in 1867, it became royal again: the Austrian imperial couple Franz Joseph I and Elisabeth (Sisi) were

Oriental flair in Rudas Thermal Bath, one of Budapest's nicest baths

crowned, making them King and Queen of Hungary. The entrance fee is hefty but well worth it; the inside of this 700-year old church is just as impressive as the outside. If you're looking for a new motif for your next panoramic shot of Budapest, then climb up the 80 m/262 ft ☀ bell tower. You will be rewarded with a magnificent bird's eye view. *Mon–Fri 9am–5pm, Sat 9am–noon, Sun 1pm–5pm | I | Szentháromság tér | www.matyas-templom.hu | bus 16, 16A, 116*

11 RUDAS THERMAL BATHS (RUDAS FÜRDŐ) (124 B4–5) (*ØØ C11*)

This Turkish domed building dating from 1556 is situated at the foot of Gellért Hill. The beautiful baths with a pool dating from 1896 have been comprehensively restored and modernised. The 450 year old steam bath is a master piece of Ot-

toman architecture and transports the visitor into another world. Particularly unusual are the nocturnal bathing times on the weekend when, by the way, both, men and women are allowed to enter. During the week there is a strict separation of genders. *Mon, Wed–Fri 6am–8pm (men only), Tue 6am–8pm (women only), Sat–Sun 6am–8pm, night swimming (no sauna) Fri, Sat 10pm–4am (mixed) | I | Döbrentei tér 9 | www.en.rudasfurdo.hu | tram 19, 41, 56, 56A | bus 7*

12 HUNGARIAN NATIONAL GALLERY (MAGYAR NEMZETI GALÉRIA) ★ (127 D5) (*ØØ B9*)

Be warned: You can literally spend hours in the National Gallery, home to the largest public collection of Hungarian fine art. If you don't have so much time (or energy) to spare, concentrate on the section exhibiting INSIDER TIP works by Mihály Munkácsy (1844–1900). Hungarians are proud of the only Hungarian-born painter to have earned international acclaim. Among the permanent exhibits are Gothic wooden sculptures, panel paintings and late-Gothic winged altars (more exciting than they sound!).

If you have made the trip here, it's worth visiting the museum shop where you can buy an excellent painting book about the National Gallery and its treasures, entitled "A colourful journey in the Hungarian National Gallery" by Viola Varga. It also sells *POPpins,* fun badges by designer Ramóna Udvardi, which are great to take back home as souvenirs. *Tue–Sun 10am–6pm | I | Szent György tér 2 | Buda Castle wings A, B, C and D | www.mng.hu | funicular | bus 16, 16A, 116*

DISTRICTS V & XIII

So much magnificence on just 6.4 sq miles! Almost all of District V (Belváros-Lipótváros) is made up of listed buildings. It is home to some of Hungary's most outstanding attractions, among them the massive Parliament Building.

Wealth, both sacred and profane, is on show in the magnificent buildings near the Parliament Building, including the monumental St Stephen's Basilica. One example of luxurious hotel architecture is the Gresham Palace, housed in a wonderful Art Nouveau building.

District V, the heart of Pest, has 27,000 inhabitants, of which 27 percent are over the age of 65. After a long period of neglect, the city centre of Pest has witnessed a remarkable resurgence thanks to substantial investment: its squares have been renovated, whole sections of roads have been closed to traffic and cafés and restaurants invite you in. The city district is becoming a popular place to go out in the evening.

To the north is District XIII (Újlipótváros, population: 113,500), of which Margaret Island, the city's green lung, is part. It also has streets with 19th-century townhouses, but it is characterised by working-class tenements and many national minorities.

■ DANUBE CORSO (DUNAKORZÓ)
   ⚓ (124 B–C 1–3) (*Ø C–D 9–10*)
It's time to don your best outfit including an extravagant hat and take up

FIT IN THE CITY

On your marks, get set, go – *Margaret Island* is the most popular address for jogging in the city. The 5.5 km/3.4 mile trail paved in rubber matting loops around the island and offers scenic views of the Danube. There are no cars to disturb your run. Most joggers start at the south entrance to the island. Underneath the Margaret Bridge there's a free ● *outdoor fitness studio* which offers power training equipment to complete your fitness routine after your run. If you prefer to be in the water rather than next to it, contact *Budapest Canoe (tel. 30 3 00 76 45 | www.budapestcanoe.com).* They offer a variety of kayak and canoe tours to meet all needs and fluent English is spoken.

SIGHTSEEING IN DISTRICTS V & XIII

▨▨▨ Pedestrian zone

1 Danube Corso (Dunakorzó)

2 Ethnographic Museum (Néprajzi Múzeum)

3 Inner City Parish Church (Belvárosi Plébániatemplom)

4 Chain Bridge (Széchenyi lánchíd)

5 Margaret Island (Margitsziget)

6 Hungarian Parliament Building (Országház)

7 Pest Redoubt (Pesti Vigadó)

8 St Stephen's Basilica (Szent István Bazilika)

9 Shoes on the Danube bank (Cipők a Duna-parton)

10 Szabadság tér

11 Széchenyi István tér

12 Hungarian Academy of Sciences (Magyar Tudományos Akadémia)

13 University Square (Egyetem tér)

14 Váci utca

15 Vörösmarty tér

your walking stick for a stroll along Budapest's posh promenade. The Duna Korzó, or Danube Corso, stretches between Széchenyi Chain Bridge and Elizabeth Bridge and this riverside promenade in Pest is reminiscent of the extravagance of the Belle Époque era, lined with extortionately priced restaurants and hotels and imposing buildings such as the Buda Redoubt. Don't forget to take a photo of yourself posing with the bronze statuette of the "Little Princess" sitting on the railings...

2 ETHNOGRAPHIC MUSEUM (NÉPRAJZI MÚZEUM) (127 F1) (*D C7*)

Why design such a lavish building to accommodate an ethnological museum? The answer lies in the fact that the building was originally built at the end of the 19th century as the Ministry of Justice, the appearance of which had to impress. Today, the museum houses interesting exhibits about the cultural traditions of Hungarians and other ethnic groups. *Tue–Sun 10am–6pm | V | Kossuth Lajos tér 12 | www.neprajz.hu/en | metro 2: Kossuth Lajos tér | tram 2*

3 INNER CITY PARISH CHURCH (BELVÁROSI PLÉBÁNIATEMPLOM) (124 C3) (*D D10*)

Just a bit to your right, please! Perhaps the most famous anecdote surrounding this Roman Catholic Church is that there were plans at the start of the 20th century to move it by a few metres to accommodate the Elisabeth Bridge. Fortunately, an alternative plan was approved to wind the bridge around the church instead, as you can still see today. A visit to this place of worship is like stepping back in time, offering an insight into its 2000-year old history: you can see (and even go down into) the crypt from Ro-

man times, one of the frescoes dating back to the 14th century and even the Muslim prayer niche, the mihrab – a legacy to the Ottoman Empire. The church

The bronze statuette of the Little Princess on the Danube promenade

is open for free to those who come to worship. *V | Március 15. tér | www.belvarosiplebania.hu | metro 3: Ferenciek tere*

4 CHAIN BRIDGE (SZÉCHENYI LÁNCHÍD) ● (127 E–F4) (*D C9*)

Without doubt this stunning bridge is a favourite among most Budapest locals and city tourists. The best place from which to capture its full beauty on a photo is standing on the adjacent Elisabeth Bridge. It's worth taking a stroll in both directions, to Pest as well as Buda and preferably before 9am or late in the evening when most tourists have gone home (and taken their selfie sticks with them!).

The splendid St Stephen's Basilica is Budapest's largest church

⑤ MARGARET ISLAND (MARGITSZIGET) ★ ●
(128 B4–6) (🗺 C–D 3–6)

It doesn't cost a penny to visit this popular Budapest attraction and it's worth visiting by day or by night whatever the season. The island is neither Buda nor Pest, floating directly in the middle of both on the Danube. It can be reached from the north over the Árpád Bridge (not particularly pretty) and from the south over the Margaret Bridge (very pretty). Stretching 2.5km/1.5mi long and 0.5km/0.3mi wide, the island is perhaps the only place in Budapest which locals can agree on and attracts the whole spectrum of the population from after-work joggers, teenage skateboarders, tourists and expats, trendy cool types with beards to grandmas in wheelchairs. Autumn is the time to stroll amongst the falling leaves collecting chestnuts while in summer visitors get around on funny 4-wheel covered bikes known as *bringóhintós*. For old and young alike, there are pubs, clubs, restaurants, *lángos*, ice cream and candy floss, a Japanese garden and even mini zoo. Save on the admission price to the zoo by viewing the cuddly animals, including the extremely cute 'silkie' chicken, from the other side of the fencing. Other popular attractions include the outdoor Palatinus swimming pool, open-air theatre and musical fountain at the southern tip of the island. The landmark on the Margaret Island is the water tower, a listed building with ☀ viewing platform (worth climbing up even if most locals haven't). *XIII | tram 4, 6: Margaret Bridge | bus 26*

⑥ HUNGARIAN PARLIAMENT BUILDING (ORSZÁGHÁZ) ★
(127 F1) (🗺 C7–8)

"Is it for sale? How many bedrooms has it got?", was apparently what the singer of Queen, Freddie Mercury, jokingly asked in 1986 when he saw the gigantic Parliament building during a boat trip on the Danube. No surprise really – whether from water or on land, the building, designed by architect Imre Steindl (1839–1902) with its neo-Gothic elements, is a bombastic piece of architecture. Its inside is equally impressive. Among the many political ideologies represented by the Hungarian Parliament, there was perhaps none so lasting as state socialism which attached its symbolic red star to the dome (96 m/315 ft high) between 1950 and 1990. The original star is on exhibit today in the Parliament Museum. And in answer to Freddie Mercury's questions: no and 700 in total. *Ticket office in the visitors' centre daily 8am–6pm (in the winter until 4pm) | English tours daily 10am, noon, 1pm, 2pm and 3pm | admission EU-citizens 2,200 Ft., non-EU-citizens 5,400 Ft. | V | Kossuth Lajos tér | tel. 1 4 41 44 15 | www.parlament.hu | metro 2: Kossuth Lajos tér | tram 2*

7 PEST REDOUBT (PESTI VIGADÓ) (124 C2) (*ᐁ C–D9*)

Wagner, Debussy, and Liszt – all the great composers have performed in this gigantic venue, opened in 1865 as a ballroom and concert hall. The Redoubt is worth seeing if only for its ornately decorated façade and neo-Romanesque style. It's a great place to catch a concert or exhibition and there's a fantastic ⤳ panoramic terrace on floor six affording great views over the city and serving a delicious cup of coffee. *Daily 10am–7pm | V | Vigadó tér | www.vigado.hu | metro 1: Vörösmarty tér | tram 2: Vigadó tér*

8 ST STEPHEN'S BASILICA (SZENT ISTVÁN BAZILIKA) ★ ⤳ (131 E5) (*ᐁ D9*)

Construction of this enormous neoclassical church lasted from 1867 to 1906. Its dome is 96 m (315 ft) high. It collapsed in 1868 and destroyed the building, which was half-finished at the time. The church's most significant art works are the statue of Alajos Stróbl and the painting "St Stephen offers Hungary to the Virgin Mary" by Gyula Benczúr. A significant relic, the mummified hand of King Stephen, is exhibited in the basilica. The view from the dome is magnificent. You can take a lift up, after which you will also have to climb some stairs. To the right of the entrance is the way down to the treasure chambers. *V | Szent István tér | metro 1: Bajcsy-Zsilinszky út | metro 3: Arany János utca*

9 INSIDER TIP SHOES ON THE DANUBE BANK (CIPŐK A DUNA-PARTON) (127 F2) (*ᐁ C8*)

Created by sculptor Gyula Pauer, this memorial on the banks of the Danube is dedicated to the Budapest Jews who suffered mass execution by Hungarian Fascists in 1944/45. The artist lined up empty shoes made of metal on the Danube docks in honour and remembrance of those killed – an extremely thought-provoking memorial. *V | Antall József rakpart | metro 2: Kossuth Lajos tér | tram 2*

10 SZABADSÁG TÉR (131 D4) (*ᐁ D8*)

All seems peaceful at first glance on Liberty Square to the south of the Hungarian Parliament. And then seemingly out of nowhere appears the enormous obelisk with the golden Red Star on the top (1946 memorial to the Soviet Red Army), a bronze statue of Ronald Reagan (2011) and the controversial antifascist monument for the victims of the German occupation placed here in 2014. As you'll see (and make sure you do visit this monstrosity), the monument depicts Hungary as the Archangel Gabriel being attacked by a German imperial eagle. The monument was funded by the Fidesz Government and it remains a point of contention for many Hungarians (including the Hungarian association of Jewish communities) who believe the monument distorts history. Protesters were so disgusted that they erected an alternative memorial in front of it which is updated regularly. Exciting! *V | metro 2: Kossuth Lajos tér | metro 2*

⑪ SZÉCHENYI ISTVÁN TÉR
(124 B1) (*ω C9*)

This square on the Pest side of the Chain Bridge was designed by the Berlin architect Friedrich Stüler in 1864. It has greatly benefited from the wonderful renovation of the Gresham Palace, named after the London-based Gresham insurance company. The two statues on the pedestals are of the reformist Count István Széche-

LOW BUDGET

City tours for under a pound: take the *tram line 2* to experience Budapest from its best sides in everyday life (try not to go during rush hour, it gets too full). The best place to sit is on the Danube side. Line 2 takes around 20 minutes from the Pest end of Margaret Bridge along the Danube to the terminus at the Palace of Arts.

Although thrilling, sightseeing can also be exhausting stuff. If you get hungry between sights, head to the nearest restaurant and ask if they have a lunchtime or daily menu. Most restaurants serve them during the week and two or three courses are often available for just a handful of change.

nyi (1791–1860) and the statesman Ferenc Deák (1803–76). *V | tram 2 | bus 16, 105*

⑫ HUNGARIAN ACADEMY OF SCIENCES (MAGYAR TUDOMÁNYOS AKADÉMIA)
(127 F3) (*ω C8–9*)

To put it simply, this is where some of the nation's cleverest brain cells dream up really intelligent ideas, for example scientists are currently working with the carmakers Audio to develop the car of the future. Although there is not much to see inside, the striking neo-Renaissance building (dated 1862) nestled between the Danube and Gresham Palace is worth seeing. *V | Széchenyi István tér 9 | tram 2*

⑬ INSIDER TIP ▶ UNIVERSITY SQUARE (EGYETEM TÉR)
(125 E4) (*ω D–E10*)

Since it has been closed to traffic, this square in the city's south has regained a lot of its former charm. Home to the Central University Building and the Károlyi Palace, the square offers several cafés and the small park *Károlyi Kert* (see p. 107) is just a few feet away. The *University Church (Egyetemi templom)* is also located around the corner, a Baroque masterpiece from the middle of the 18th century. The delicate frescoes and the pulpit are particularly worthy of note. *V | metro 3, 4: Kálvin tér*

⑭ VÁCI UTCA
(124–125 C–D 2–5) (*ω D9–10*)

This shopping street between Vörösmarty tér, Ferenciek tere and Fővám tér is a magnet for visitors. You will find the usual international chain stores and perfumeries typical of such thoroughfares. The pedestrianised southern section all the way to Fővám tér has its own flair, with an array of interesting shops, including fashion boutiques and antique shops. *V | metro 1: Vörösmarty tér | metro 3: Ferenciek tere | metro 4: Fővám tér*

⒖ VÖRÖSMARTY TÉR
(124 C2) (ᗌ D9)

In the middle of the square is a memorial to the poet Mihály Vörösmarty (1800–55). The splendid monument is made of high-quality Carrara marble. At the front end, opposite Váci utca, is the renowned Café Gerbeaud. *V | metro 1: Vörösmarty tér*

DISTRICTS VI & XIV

District VI (Terézváros, population: 42,000) boasts a special mix of culture and trendy goings-on. The main highlight here is the boulevard Andrássy út.

High art mingles with popular culture on and around Andrássy út. There are, for example, the Opera House, the Academy of Music, the Kogart Gallery and the Operetta Theatre. The restaurant and café scene is just as lively, particularly on Liszt Ferenc tér, "Budapest's Broadway".

With Budapest's most imposing square, Heroes' Square, at the northeastern end of Andrássy út and the adjoining municipal forest, District XIV (Zugló, population: 120,000) has two of the capital's attractions to call its own.

⒈ ANDRÁSSY ÚT ★ *(131 E–F 4–5, 132 A–B 7–4) (ᗌ D–F 7–9)*

Do you realise you're trampling on a Unesco World Heritage Site? You don't need to tread carefully though – just appreciate the amazing architecture flanking this 2.5 km/1.5 mile long boulevard. Alternatively, take the underground,

known locally as *Földalatti,* which also has its charm. The tram is small, the carriages are short and the doors close so quickly that you can barely get in before they shut on you. Opened in 1896, it is the oldest underground in Europe followed by the London Underground.

Back above ground on the Andrássy út, known as the "Champs Élysées of Budapest", you pass various sections as you stroll down from your starting point at the Bajcsy-Zsilinszky út crossroads to the end at the vast Heroes' Square. Lined at the start with diverse luxury stores, you walk past the delightful Opera House and restaurants then pop up on both your left and right. From the Oktogon onwards, the avenue becomes quieter and the architecture more elegant until

Avenue of riches: the elegant Andrássy út

The House of Terror is a memorial to the victims of the heinous 20th-century regimes

it reaches the Millennium Monument where the sheer size of Heroes' Square will bowl you over.

■2 BUDAPEST ZOO (BUDAPESTI ÁLLATKERT) (132 B1–2) (*∅ F–G6*)

Located in the municipal forest, the zoo is listed as a nature preservation and cultural heritage site. Founded in 1866, it not only houses many exotic animals but also is an architectural gem with its amazing INSIDER TIP Art Nouveau buildings. Special attractions include the richly adorned elephant house – one of the most beautiful examples of Art Nouveau in Budapest – and the palm house dating back to the start of the 20th century. The colourful tiles were produced by the famous Southern Hungarian Zsolnay tile and porcelain manufacture. Entertaining open-air concerts are held in front of the palm house in summer. In 2014, the zoo took over the grounds of the former amusement park; some of its listed heritage attractions are open to visitors in summer in the *Holnemvolt Park*. *May–Aug Mon–Thu 9am–6pm, Fri–Sun 10am–7pm, otherwise daily 9am–4pm (March/Oct until 5pm, April/Sept until 5:30pm) | XIV | Állatkerti körút 6–12 | www.zoobudapest.com | metro 1: Széchenyi fürdő*

■3 HOUSE OF TERROR (TERROR HÁZA) (131 F4) (*∅ E8*)

The House of Terror is a memorial to the victims of 20th-century persecution, illustrating the grim decades of Jewish and Roma persecution under the Nazis and further repression and misery under the Communists. It is housed in the very building where, from 1937 onwards, the grisly Nazi secret police established their headquarters. Countless people were physically and psychologically broken, tortured to death, or executed in the building's basement. After the end of World War II, the Hungarian secret service and security organisations took over

SIGHTSEEING IN DISTRICTS VI & XIV

1 Andrássy út

2 Budapest Zoo (Budapesti Állatkert)

3 House of Terror (Terror háza)

4 Heroes' Square (Hősök tere)

5 Kogart (Kogart Ház)

6 Liszt Ferenc tér

7 Museum of Fine Arts (Szépművészeti Múzeum)

8 Oktogon

9 Opera House (Operaház)

10 Municipal forest (Városliget)

▨▨▨ Pedestrian zone

11 Széchenyi Baths (Széchenyi fürdő)

12 Vajdahunyad Castle (Vajdahunyadvár)

the premises, torturing, executing or deporting poeple to soviet camps. *Tue–Sun 10am–6pm | VI | Andrássy út 60 | www.terrorhaza.hu | metro 1: Oktogon | tram 4, 6*

4 HEROES' SQUARE (HŐSÖK TERE) ★
(132 B2) (*Ⓜ G6*)

Heroes' Square, on the northeastern end of Andrássy út, is the city's largest square and combines national pride with aesthetics to produce a successful whole. The 36-m (121 ft) column in the middle of the square, the Millennium Memorial, commemorates the 1,000th anniversary of the creation of the Hungarian nation in 896. In 1896, the parliament decided to commission a monument, but 33 years passed before it was finally completed in 1929. Archangel Gabriel stands up on the column. He allegedly ordered King Stephen in a dream to convert Hungary to Christianity; today he watches skateboarders zooming over the square. The statues in the two colonnade arches are of heroes of Hungary's history. The square's other central elements are two classical monuments: the Hall of Art and the Museum of Fine Arts. *XIV | metro 1: Hősök tere | bus 30*

5 INSIDER TIP KOGART (KOGART HÁZ) ● (132 B3) (*F6*)

This beautifully renovated villa near the municipal forest is a feast for the eyes. It houses the art collection of Gábor Kovács, a successful investment banker. His passion is for 19th- and 20th-century Hungarian art. *Mon–Fri 10am–6pm | VI | Andrássy út 112 | www.kogart.hu | metro 1: Bajza utca*

6 LISZT FERENC TÉR ● (131 F4) (*E8*)

This 200 m/656 ft long square centres around a green strip of park area and is flanked by cafes and restaurants: more a street than a conventional square, the Liszt Ferenc tér is a secluded corner in this otherwise bustling area of the city centre. Named after the piano virtuoso and composer Franz Liszt (1811–86), the square commemorates him with two statues – one in the middle erected in 1986 on the 100th anniversary of his death and a bronze statuette on the splendid Liszt Ferenc Music Academy on the corner of Király utca. Order a coffee or ice cream in one of the establishments and watch the comings and goings. *VI | metro 1: Oktogon | tram 4, 6*

7 MUSEUM OF FINE ARTS (SZÉPMŰVÉSZETI MÚZEUM) ● (132 B2) (*F–G6*)

If you prefer classic to contemporary, then this museum is for you. The museum building is 100 years old but its collection dates back further with Egyptian, Greek and Roman artefacts and a large selection of Italian paintings. In the past, it has housed internationally acclaimed exhibitions from Picasso to Toulouse-Lautrec. Please consult the website before you visit to check that the extensive renovations have been completed. Up until then, around 50 works of art are

SPOTLIGHT ON SPORTS

Attention, Formula 1 fans: the Hungarian Grand Prix takes place at the *Hungaroring (12 miles northeast of the city centre | www.hungaroring.hu)* at the beginning of August. Almost 80 percent of the track can be seen from the stands. Budapest also hosts major running events several times a year. In September and October the city attracts thousands of runners and tens of thousands of spectators and partygoers.

The *Wizz Air Budapest Half Marathon* and the *Spar Budapest Marathon* both start from Heroes' Square *(www.budapestmarathon.com)*.
The football club *Fradi* (FTC/Ferencváros Torna Club from 1899) *(IX | Üllői út 129 | www.fradi.hu | metro 3: Nagyvárad tér)* enjoys cult status. Legendary players of this green-and-white team (Hungarian champions 29 times) were Flórián Albert and Tibor Nyilasi, to name but two.

The Opera's dazzling golden auditorium can also be visited by guided tour

on temporary display in the Castle Palace. *Tue–Sun 10am–6pm | XIV | Dózsa György út 41 | www.szepmuveszeti.hu |metro 1: Hősök tere | bus 30*

8 OKTOGON (131 F4) (*m E8*)

Situated at the intersection of Andrássy útca and Térez körút, this octagonal square is among Budapest's most attractive representative squares, lined by 19th-century apartment blocks. *VI | metro 1: Oktogon*

9 OPERA HOUSE (OPERAHÁZ) ●
(131 E5) (*m D–E8*)

The magnificent Neo-Renaissance building, constructed between 1875 and 1884, is a work by the architect Miklos Ybl, who also drew up the plans for the entire Andrássy út. It is not just the opera's façade that is stunningly beautiful, but the opulent interior as well. *English-language tours every day at 3pm and 4pm (www.operavisit.hu), no pre-booking necessary | VI | Andrássy út 22 | www.opera.hu | metro 1: Opera*

10 MUNICIPAL FOREST (VÁROSLIGET)
(132–133 C–D 2–3) (*m G–H 6–7*)

The extensive park is dotted with interesting attractions such as Vajdahunyad, the "fairytale castle" and Budapest Zoo. A hit among teenagers is the **INSIDER TIP** *ice rink (Nov–March Mo, Tue 9am–1pm and 5pm–8pm, Wed–Fri 9am–1pm and 4pm–8pm, Sat, Sun 10am–2pm and 4pm–8pm | Olof Palme sétány 5 | www.mujegpalya.hu)*. During the summer it is a lake on which you can go canoeing. Gourmets will be attracted to the famous Gundel restaurant, while the *Széchenyi Baths* appeal to spa fans. *XIV | metro 1: Hősök tere and Széchenyi fürdő | trolleybus 72*

11 SZÉCHENYI BATHS
(SZÉCHENYI FÜRDŐ) ●
(132 C1–2) (*m G6*)

These baths resemble a magnificent palace complex. There are twelve indoor and three outdoor pools. The day clinic offers a broad range of treatments, but the baths are also popular among the fully fit and healthy. It is simply great fun to sit in one of the open-air pools and enjoy the warm thermal water or to get in shape in the fitness suite. You'll need a bit of luck to get a spot by one of the chessboards in the pools, however. The spa treatments on offer include Thai massages and foot massages as well as workouts. *Pools daily 6am–10pm, other facilities until 4pm or 7pm | XIV | Állatkerti körút 11 | www.szechenyibad.hu | metro 1: Széchenyi fürdő*

▣ VAJDAHUNYAD CASTLE (VAJDA-HUNYADVÁR) ● (132 C2) (ᗡ *G6*)

This medieval-looking castle in the municipal forest was built in the 19th cen-

Imaginative architecture in the municipal forest: Vajdahunyad Castle

tury. The architect took his inspiration from Hungary's traditional architectural styles. The castle houses a large agricultural museum, but it is visited not just for its exhibits: the magnificently furnished rooms are also well worth seeing. In summer the courtyard is transformed into a wonderful stage for lively summer concerts. The people of Budapest love their fantasy castle beyond measure. *Museum April–Oct Tue–Sun 10am–5pm, otherwise Tue–Fri 10am–4pm, Sat/Sun until 5pm | www.mmgm.hu | XIV | Vajdahunyad sétány | metro 1: Széchenyi fürdő*

DISTRICTS VII & VIII

Goszdu Court is not the only hip spot along the Király utca. The trendy street is administratively still part of district VI, but it's also the starting point for discovering district VII (Erzsébetváros, population: 62,500) with the old Jewish Quarter.

As well as providing reminders of the past, District VII is all about optimism for the future. This part of the city used to be dominated by Jewish life and faith, particularly between Király utca and Dohány utca. Today, it is well on its way to combining tradition and modernity. Be they cool designer shops or kosher restaurants, hip bars or shops selling Jewish religious artefacts, magnificently restored houses or still visible decay: the trendy quarter developing here has its own very special flair. The district is also associated with the development of Hungarian literature, inextricably linked with the coffee house New York. The successor glows in its former glory, but literary figures are however no longer seen here. The young scene meets in

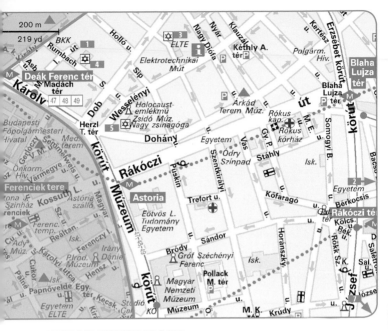

SIGHTSEEING IN DISTRICTS VII & VIII

1 Gozsdu Court (Gozsdu udvar)

2 Kerepesi Cemetery
(Kerepesi temető)

3 Orthodox Synagogue (Ortodox zsinagóga)

4 Rumbach Synagogue
(Rumbach Sebestyén utcai zsinagóga)

5 Dohány Street Synagogue
(Dohány utcai zsinagóga)

6 Hungarian National Museum
(Magyar Nemzeti Múzeum)

7 Hungarian Natural History
Museum (Magyar Természettudományi Múzeum)

the popular "ruin pubs" of the former Jewish quarter.

District VIII (Józsefváros/Joseph Town, 82,000 inhabitants) was home to the literary elite of the country in the 1930s and also covers an extensive working class quarter. A few years ago it made the headlines as a social flashpoint, but things are now changing. That holds particularly true for the student oriented "Palace quarter" around the National Museum. Anyone wanting to see the modernisation process for themselves should explore a few of the streets around Gutenberg tér (near Blaha Lujza

tér). Among the rows of houses there are some wonderfully restored buildings. Between them, however, are some that still look just like they did after the war.

1 **INSIDER TIP** **GOZSDU COURT**
(GOZSDU UDVAR) (125 E1) (*Ø E9*)
Gozsdu Court on the edge of the old Jewish Quarter is an architectural masterpiece which runs from Király utca 13 to Dob utca. The imposing 19th-century complex consists of seven buildings and six interlinking courtyards. Visitors can stroll from one courtyard to the next. Many nice restaurants and cafés

Lively hotspot in the Jewish Quarter: Gozsdu Court is the place to celebrate in the evenings

have settled in the longish complex of buildings and turned Gozsdu Court into a lively hotspot. *VII | Király utca 13/Dob utca 16 | www.gozsduudvar.hu | metro 1, 2, 3: Deák Ferenc tér*

2 KEREPESI CEMETERY (KEREPESI TEMETŐ)
(137 D–E1) (*Ⓜ H–J 9–10*)

Several important 19th-century politicians are buried in this famous cemetery with its parkland setting and many ancient trees. Lajos Kossuth, the activist during the Hungarian Revolution of 1848, has an imposing mausoleum. Nearby is a memorial dating from the communist era, where "worthy fighters" were laid to rest. Poets and thinkers also lie buried here, including the novelist Jókai Mór (1825–1904, lot 18) and the poet Ady Endre (1877–1919, lot 19/1). At the eastern edge of the cemetery, with its tree-lined avenues, is a

decaying Jewish cemetery with impressive mausoleums. *During summer daily 7am–8pm, during winter 7:30am–5pm | VIII | Fiumei út 16 | metro 2, 4: Keleti pályaudvar | tram 24, 28*

3 ORTHODOX SYNAGOGUE (ORTODOX ZSINAGÓGA)
(131 F5) (*Ⓜ E9*)

One of the three large synagogues in the Jewish District was erected in Art Nouveau style between 1911 and 1913 for the Jewish Orthodox community.Because of its address, it is also known as the Kazinczy Street Synagogue and you can find many Jewish buildings and stores situated around the synagogue. It has been lovingly restored and can house up to 1000 worshippers. *During summer Sun–Thu 10am–6pm, Fri 10am–4pm, during winter Sun–Thu 10am–4pm, Fri 10am–2pm | VII | Kazinczy utca 29–31 | metro 2: Astoria*

4 RUMBACH SYNAGOGUE (RUMBACH SEBESTYÉN UTCAI ZSINAGÓGA)
(125 E1) (𝄐 E9)

This "little synagogue", an early work by the Viennese Art Nouveau architect Otto Wagner (1841–1918), has not yet been restored, but it is occasionally open to the public in the summer months. *VII | Rumbach Sebestyén utca 11–13 | metro 1, 2, 3: Deák Ferenc tér*

5 DOHÁNY STREET SYNAGOGUE (DOHÁNY UTCAI ZSINA-GÓGA) ★ ● (125 E2) (𝄐 E9)

This place of worship with its onion domes was built in the mid-19th century in the Byzantine-Moorish style. It is the largest synagogue in Europe and is one of the city's most magnificent buildings. In its courtyard, where the *Holocaust Memorial* by the sculptor Imre Varga is located – a silver, shimmering tree of life – thousands of victims of fascism lie buried. One of the wings houses the *Jewish Museum (Zsidó Múzeum | www.zsidomuseum.hu)*, which has a rich collection of Judaica ranging from Roman times to the 20th century. On the site of the present-day museum stood the house where Theodor Herzl (1860–1904), the founder of Zionism, was born. *March–Oct Sun–Thu 10am–6pm, Fri 10am–3:30pm (April–Oct until 4:30pm), otherwise Sun–Thu 10am–4pm, Fri 10am–2pm | VII | Dohány utca 2 | www.dohanystreetsynagogue.hu | metro 2: Astoria | tram 47, 49*

6 HUNGARIAN NATIONAL MUSEUM (MAGYAR NEMZETI MÚZEUM) ★
(125 F4) (𝄐 E10)

Take a moment before entering the museum to admire the building from the outside with its splendid gardens and broad flight of steps – a popular spot for students from the nearby elite university and ideal for a quick coffee before you start on the vast exhibition inside. Opened in 1847, this museum houses an immense collection of artefacts and relics. The best is to start in the basement and work your way up through the various eras in Hungarian history. Most visitors particularly enjoy the period exhibition from the end of World War II to the fall of communism. The museum is immensely proud to own the coronation mantle of King Stephen, Hungary's first king. *Tue–Sun 10am–6pm | VIII | Múzeum körút 14–16 | www.mnm.hu | metro 3, 4: Kálvin tér | tram 47, 48, 49*

7 HUNGARIAN NATURAL HISTORY MUSEUM (MAGYAR TERMÉSZET-TUDOMÁNYI MÚZEUM)
(136 C3) (𝄐 H12)

The neoclassical museum complex is a fascinating place. The glass floor leading up to the exhibition lets visitors look down on coral reefs, while a 3-ton skeleton of a fin whale hangs from the domed ceiling of the entrance foyer. The "Treasures of the Carpathian Basin" collection brings a world of myths and legends to life. *Wed–Mon 10am–6pm | VIII | Ludovika tér 2–6 | www.nhmus.hu | metro 3: Klinikák*

DISTRICT IX

District IX (Ferencváros, population: 61,500) has undergone a revival. Its central attraction is Ráday utca with its cafés, restaurants, boutiques and book and music shops.

The city's young and young at heart like coming here because Ráday utca and the surrounding area have good, affordable living space as well. At the southern end of this district is a project

DISTRICT IX

which, when completed, will confirm the reputation of this part of town as the capital's new cultural centre: the Millennium Quarter with the National Theatre and the Palace of Arts. District IX has its sunny sides, but there is still a lot of work to be done, particularly in the southern residential neighbourhoods. Around 300 houses need demolishing, while 2,500 still have to be renovated.

■ LIBERTY BRIDGE (SZABADSÁG HÍD) ● (125 D6) (*⫽ D11*)

"Let's meet up on the Bridge," is often the phrase you hear from students and young people in Budapest when the summer evenings become longer. What they mean is the green cantilevered *szabi-híd* as the locals like to call their Liberty Bridge. Crowds gather in the

middle of the bridge where the metal construction is low enough to sit on and enjoy the picturesque views over the Gellért Hill and Liberty Statue. Inaugurated in 1896, Liberty Bridge is closed to car traffic and public transport at certain weekends in summer for picnic revellers, musicians, acrobats, longboard skaters, hammock enthusiasts and open-air cinema fans to come and hangout. What a great sense of liberty!

■ INSIDER TIP ▶ HOLOCAUST MEMORIAL CENTER (HOLOKAUSZTEMLÉKÖZ-PONT) (136 B3) (*⫽ F12*)

This complex is worth seeing for its architecture alone. It consists of the historic Páva Synagogue and a new wing dominated by glass. The interior deals with something much darker: the Holocaust in Hungary. In spring 1944,

Liberty Bridge for everyone: popular hangout in summer

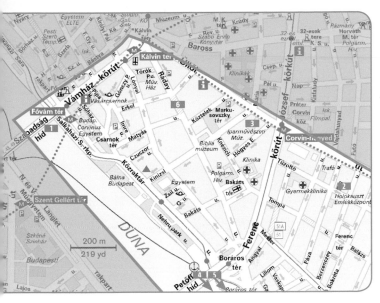

SIGHTSEEING IN DISTRICT IX

1 Liberty Bridge (Szabadság híd)

2 Holocaust Memorial Center (Holokauszt Emlékközpont)

3 Museum of Applied Arts (Iparművészeti Múzeum)

4 Ludwig Museum (Ludwig Múzeum)

5 Palace of Arts (Művészetek Palotája)

6 Ráday utca

░░░ Pedestrian zone

---

under the rule of Regent Miklós Horthy, 440,000 people were deported to Auschwitz. The Germans and the Arrow Cross Party (the Hungarian Nazis), who came to power in autumn 1944, were responsible for the deaths of tens of thousands more people. In total, the number of murdered Hungarian Jews and Roma is estimated at more than 600,000. Darkness, the light in the cabinets, nightmarish sounds such as the footsteps of concentration camp guards: the exhibition is a journey from darkness to the synagogue's light domed room and out into the light of day. It recalls the warning motto "principiis obsta", "nip it in the bud". *Tue–Sun 10am–6pm | IX | Páva utca 39 | www.hdke.hu | metro 3: Corvin-negyed | tram 4, 6*

3 MUSEUM OF APPLIED ARTS (IPARMŰVÉSZETI MÚZEUM)
(136 A3) *(ω F11)*

The building is currently closed for renovation and is expected to be finished by 2019 – so make sure you check out its website before planning a visit. Although the exhibits inside are not everyone's cup of tea anyway, the building is worth a sneak peek for its magnificent Art Nouveau architecture with green ceramic tiled roof, an elegant pure white atrium in the entrance area and oriental details. *IX | Üllöi út 33–37 | www.imm.hu | metro 3: Corvin negyed | tram 4, 6*

◆ LUDWIG MUSEUM (LUDWIG MÚZEUM) (136 A6) (*ΩΩ F14*)

Ever considered getting an electric shock from a work of art? Curious to see some

Dazzling green and yellow Majolica tiles decorate the roof of the Museum of Applied Arts

post-Soviet installation art? Or how about photo exhibitions about the beat generation? What's sure is boredom is not an issue in the Ludwig Museum with its ever-changing exhibitions which are invariably well received. Budapest owes this important collection of contemporary international art to the collectors Irene and Peter Ludwig from Aachen in Germany. *Tue–Sun 10am–8pm | IX | Komor Marcell utca 1 | www.ludwigmuseum. hu | tram 2, 24*

◆ PALACE OF ARTS (MŰVÉSZETEK PALOTÁJA) (136 A6) (*ΩΩ F14*)

With its large glass window façade, the Palace of Arts is an impressive piece of contemporary architecture. If you can't manage to catch a concert in the Béla Bartók National Concert Hall or an exhibition at the Ludwig Museum for Contemporary Art, take a walk to see the INSIDER TIP snail sculpture in front of the palace or enjoy a stroll along the Danube. *IX | Komor Marcell utca 1 | www. mupa.hu | tram 2, 24*

◆ RÁDAY UTCA (125 F5–6) (*ΩΩ E11–12*)

The traffic-calmed pedestrian zone Ráday utca, which has become a popular destination because of its many cafés and restaurants, begins at Kálvin tér. *Metro 3, 4: Kálvin tér | tram 47, 48, 49*

IN OTHER DISTRICTS

KIRÁLY BATHS (KIRÁLY FÜRDŐ) (130 C3) (*ΩΩ B7*)

Although small in size, the Király Baths are for many locals the prettiest thermal baths in Budapest due to their authentic Turkish influences (they were built in 1565 under the orders of Pasa Arslan). The most famous feature is the skylit central dome above the thermal pool. There is also a steam room, sauna and massage parlour but no proper swimming pool. *Daily 7am–9pm | II | Fő utca 84 | www.kiralyfurdo.hu | bus 109 Kacsa utca*

MEMENTO PARK (138 C5) *(m O)*

How small you feel in comparison to the great figures of communism (Marx, Engels, Lenin) and other monuments of socialist realism which have been relocated from around the city to their final resting place here. This outdoor sculpture park also includes an old Trabant car (photo opportunity!), an iconic symbol of the collapse of the Eastern Bloc. There is also an indoor exhibition which provides more historic background information. Despite its distance from the city centre, it is a great place to visit if you're interested in relics and oddities from the communist era. *Daily 10am–sunset | XXII | corner Balatoni út/Szabadkai utca | www.mementopark.hu | bus 101, 150 from station and metro station Kelenföld vasútállomás (Mon–Fri approx. every 10 mins, Sat/Sun every 30 mins) or free shuttle bus from Deák Square (near the metro, daily 11am, return journey at 1pm) | tickets for a programme with a guided tour are available on the bus*

PÁLVÖLGYI CAVE AND SZEMLŐHEGYI CAVE (PÁLVÖLGYI BARLANG/SZEMLŐHEGYI BARLANG)
● (138 C4) *(m O)*

These caves with their mineral and stalactite formations are a piece of real, fascinating nature. They are 800 m (half a mile) apart. It is cold in both caves (11 degrees), so it is a good idea to wear warm clothes and stout footwear. *Pálvölgyi Cave (II | Szépvölgyi út 162 | bus 65 from Kolosy tér to the stop Pálvölgyi cseppkőbarlang)* is the city's longest cave system, measuring 29 km (18 miles) in length; 500 m (1,650 ft) of it can be visited as part of a guided tour (no access for children under five). The 300 m (985 ft) of *Szemlőhegyi Cave (II | Pusztaszeri út 35 | www.dunaipoly.hu/en | bus 29 from Kolosy tér to Pálvölgyi Cave)* are easier to contend with. *Guided tours for both caves run all year round Tue–Thu 10am–4pm on the hour*

TÜRBE OF GÜL BABA (GÜL BABA TÜRBEJE) ● ⚱ (130 B2) *(m B6)*

For many Hungarians the period under Ottoman rule is still an uncomfortable chapter in their history – and yet, from today's perspective, it was a fruitful period

FROM MOSCOW WITH LOVE

"Next stop: Moszkv- er, Széll Kálmán tér!" Despite being renamed years ago, you can still hear bus drivers calling the square in District II by its old name. In 2011, the Mayor of Budapest István Tarlós (Fidesz Party) thought the time had come for fresh political wind in the city and renamed dozens of squares, streets and bridges – yet locals were not so easily persuaded and the main intersection in Buda is and always will be their *Moszkva tér* (Moscow Square). The square carried the name for over 60 years and was even the title of one of the most popular films in Hungary directed by Ferenc Török about the days of the collapse of the Eastern bloc. So the name stays and seems to prove that the Hungarians are melancholic, nostalgic folk not prepared to easily forget the past.

rich in treasures such as this magnificent tomb in honour of Gül Baba, an Ottoman Bektashi dervish who came to Hungary with the Turkish army. After his death in 1541, Sultan Suleiman the Magnificent declared him the patron saint of Buda. The tomb lies at the foot of Rózsadomb (Rose Hill) and is the most northerly pilgrimage site for Muslims. It is a great place to unwind affording splendid views and appropriately smells of roses in spring and summer seeing that Gül Baba is known as the "Father of Roses". The easiest way to get there is from the Margit híd budai hídfő tram stop: walk up Margit körút, Margit utca and Mecset utca to the steps at the end which lead to the tomb. A more romantic route is from the corner of Frankel Leó út/Török utca: walk up the steep, cobblestoned Gül Baba utca; it's best to leave your flip-flops and high heels back in the hotel. II | Mecset utca 14

OUTSIDE THE CITY

BUDA HILLS (BUDAI-HEGYSÉG)
(138 B–C 4–5) (*Ω O*)

Straight from the city into the hills: The *cog railway (Fogaskerekűvasút)* dating from 1874 takes around half an hour to get to the top of *Széchenyi-hegy*. Those of an active disposition can walk up to *János-hegy* (527 m/1,729 ft), the highest peak of the Buda Hills: first, walk along the *childrens' railway (Gyermekvasút)* to the Normafa stop, from there via Eötvös út and Jánoshegyi út up to the top station of the *chairlift (Libegő)* (approx. 45 minutes). The hill is crowned by the stone ⚤ INSIDER TIP▶ *Elisabeth tower*. On clear days visibility can be up to 50 miles! Those who do not feel like walking the whole way can take the cog railway

to the end and then transfer to the childrens' railway getting out at the János-hegy stop. From there, a signposted hiking trail leads upwards (approx. 20 minutes). There is also the chair lift *(Libegö)* that goes up Jánoshegy in 15 minutes from the Zugliget district. Near the bottom station there is the attractive campsite *Zugligeti Niche Camping (www.camping niche.hu)* and a place that is meaningful to Germans: in 1989 Imre Kozma, a priest and the former head of the Hungarian Order of Malta, built a camp for people fleeing East Germany near Szarvas Gábor út. *Cog railway (BKK line 60) 5am–11pm from the bottom station Városmajor on Szilágyi Erzsébet fasor, can be reached from Széll Kálmán tér by tram 59 or 61 (two stops) | bottom station chairlift: Zugligeti út | from Nyugati pályaudvar with bus 291 (doesn't go via Széll Kálmán tér)*

GÖDÖLLŐ PALACE (GÖDÖLLŐI KIRÁLYI KASTÉLY) (139 F3) (*Ω O*)

The Austrian Empress and Hungarian Queen Elisabeth (Sisi) lived often in Gödöllő Palace. She loved this place, which had been made available to her and her husband, Franz Joseph I, in 1867. Its history began when Prince Antal Grassalkovich made the small village of Gödöllő the centre of his estates in the 18th century. The palace's construction began in around 1740. It is the largest Baroque structure in Hungary. Today Gödöllő (30 km/18 miles northeast of Budapest) is a town, and the palace and its park are right at the heart of it. The *Palace Museum (April–Oct daily 10am–6pm, Nov–mid-Jan and mid-Feb–March Mon–Fri 10am–4pm, Sat/Sun 10am–5pm | www.kiralyikastely.hu)* has a 170 sq m/1,830 sq ft hall, Sisi's chambers and Hungary's only Baroque theatre. Events and concerts are held at the palace. There is a fine café on the ground floor. *Suburban train/HÉV H8 from Örs vezér tere (terminus of metro 2), get off at Szabadság tér in Gödöllő*

SZENTENDRE (139 D2–3) *(⌀ 0)*

This lovely town is situated 20 km (12 miles) north of Budapest on the Danube Bend. Szentendre saw a large number

constructed in 1752–54. Only a few steps away is the fine *Margit Kovács Museum (daily | Vastagh György utca 1),* which displays the works by the famous ceramicist (1902–77). There are some great views from ⚜ *Castle Hill,* which is also the location of Szentendre's oldest church *(Római Katolikus Plébániatemplom).* Just 3 km (2

Hungary's largest Baroque palace: Gödöllő Palace was Empress Sisi's favourite

of creative individuals move here at the start of the 20th century. The *Ferenczy Múzeum (Kossuth Lajos utca 5)* between the town's train station and old city offers an insight into the history of this colony of artists as well as the artworks of the influential Ferenczy family. The town's seven orthodox churches were built by Serbian immigrants who had fled from the Turks. The narrow streets and the houses built close together are also characteristic features. On the *main square (Fő tér)* you can see a valuable wrought-iron *Memorial Cross* of 1752 and *Blagovescenska Church,*

miles) northwest of Szentendre is Hungary's largest ethnographic museum, the *Skanzen (April–Oct Tue–Sun 9am–5pm, Nov, Feb–March Sat/Sun 10am–4pm | Sztravodai út | www.skanzen.hu)* with several settlements, three churches, a windmill, a historic railway and much more. *Museums in Szentendre spring–autumn mostly Tue–Sun 10am–6pm | www.muzeumicentrum. hu | information Szentendre: Tourinform (Dumtsa Jenő utca 22 | tel. 26 31 79 65 | szentendre@tourinform.hu) | suburban train/HÉV H5 (trains every 40 minutes from Batthyány ter) | boat from Vigadó tér*

FOOD & DRINK

A Hungarian saying is "The best is to eat when you're hungry" so think about bringing a healthy appetite with you when you visit Budapest.

The city caters for every taste and size of appetite with everything from charming, nostalgic coffee houses to modern food temples. By the way, don't take the word "coffee house" too literally. Almost all of Budapest's coffeehouses and cafés are also restaurants.

Hungarians like to eat their hearts out. Lard and cream are not frowned upon, because the food is meant to taste nice after all, regardless of the calories. Among the popular traditional dishes are breaded meat or fish as well as goulash dishes, which are called *pörkölt*, *paprikás* or *tokány*. Since the country is rich in wildlife, almost every menu will also have game dishes.

Hungarians are proud of their culinary traditions and quite resistant towards foreign influences. But change is visibly afoot everywhere, particularly in Budapest. International trends are having an impact and ambitious Hungarian chefs are discovering lighter versions of their local cuisine. They are also focusing more and more on the good meat quality of old Hungarian breeds such as Mangalica pigs and grey cattle.

Paprika plays a central role in Hungarian cooking. The spice gives the dishes a characteristic, but mostly moderate heat. Just a few of the fresh chilli peppers served on the side or as part of a salad can be very hot indeed.

Photo: Stew with potatoes and peppers

From gourmet temples to street food in the party district: Budapest's culinary scene is getting more and more interesting

A pleasing development has taken place when it comes to wine. Some typical varieties are Kékfrankos, Kékoportó and Kadarka. More and more better wines of the Merlot, Pinot Noir and Cabernet Franc varieties are coming on to the market. The wines from the famous wine-growing region of Tokaj-Hegyalja are exquisite, and the dessert wines Tokaj Aszú especially so. The herbal bitter *Unicum*, sold in the striking round bottle, and the fruit brandies *(pálinka)* are served as a digestif after almost every Hungarian meal.

COFFEEHOUSES & CAFÉS

INSIDER TIP ANJUNA ICE POPS
(131 D5) (*D9*)

Ice pops with a variety of exotic flavours such as mango and avocado-tarragon-lime as well as masala chai-chocolate and litchi rose, caffè latte with matcha, açai bowls and raw cakes made of coconut and raspberry: sounds delicious, right? Anjuna is constantly creating new ice cream specialities to take away – all made from 100% natural ingredients, with no artificial colours or flavourings, suitable for vegans as well as gluten and lactose-free. *Daily | V | Sas utca 7 | www.anjunapops.com | metro 3: Arany János utca*

beautiful, old style but with a pleasant and relaxed atmosphere. This former haunt for the country's literary elite had to close at the end of World War II. Today the café with its high, lofty ceilings

Grandeur in true Budapest tradition: the New York Kávéház

AUGUSZT ⊕ (125 E3) (*𝑀 D10*)

Organic milk, butter and eggs are used for the delicious cake creations in this long-established café. The excellent quality of the ingredients turns the cakes and ice creams here into exquisite treats that can be enjoyed at the bistro tables. Nice branch in Buda. *Closed Sun | V | Kossuth Lajos utca 14–16 | metro 3: Ferenciek tere; branch: (130 A3) (f A7) (I | Fény utca 8 | metro 2: Széll Kálmán tér); www.auguszt cukraszda.hu*

CENTRÁL KÁVÉHÁZ (125 E4) (*𝑀 D10*)

Budapest cheered when this long-established café was re-opened: in a

attracts mainly tourists – it's worth just popping in for a look. *Daily | V | Károlyi Mihály utca 9 | www.centralkavehaz.hu | metro 3: Ferenciek tere*

INSIDER TIP ▶ CSÉSZÉNYI KÁVÉZÓ ÉS PÖRKÖLŐ (126 C4) (*𝑀 A9*)

Unknown to many, the Csészényi in Buda is a delightfully cosy café with mouthwatering coffee and cake specialties all made from natural ingredients without any additives. One of the walls is covered with old hand-held coffee grinders and older locals like coming here to read their newspapers in peace. A good time is guaranteed! *Dai-*

ly | I | Krisztina körút 34 | www.cseszenyi. hu | tram 41, 56 | bus 105

GERBEAUD (124 C2) (𝔐 D9)

Admittedly, the Gerbeaud is overpriced but worth it alone for its mouthwatering cream cheese-filled pastries. The French pastry chef and chocolatier Emil Gerbeaud took over the legendary coffeehouse from his Hungarian colleague in 1884. This traditional establishment oozes nostalgic charm from the interior and exterior design to the enchanting old-school waiters. No wonder that a 15% tip is automatically added to the total amount on the bill. *Daily | V | Vörösmarty tér 7–8 | www.gerbeaud.hu | metro 1: Vörösmarty tér*

JEDERMANN (135 F3) (𝔐 E11)

The Goethe Institute is still there, but the old Café Eckermann is now the Jedermann. The new owner Hans van Vliet is an amateur jazz musician and often offers live jazz and folk music in the evenings. After breakfast, the relaxed café, situated at the bottom end of Ráday utca, offers cheap lunch menus. *Daily | IX | Ráday utca 58 | www.jedermann.hu | metro 3: Corvin-negyed | tram 2, 4, 6 Boraros tér*

NEW YORK KÁVÉHÁZ ★ ●
(132 A5) (𝔐 F9)

The Neo-baroque magnificence of this legendary café is breathtaking. Other cafés are cosier, but to have a coffee in such stylish surroundings or to enjoy a piece of cake or a fruit shake here are experiences not to be missed! *Daily | VII | Erzsébet körút 9–11 | www.newyorkcafe. hu | metro 2: Blaha Lujza tér | tram 4, 6*

SZATYOR BÁR ÉS GALÉRIA
(135 D4) (𝔐 D12)

This brightly furnished café bar brings a fresh new look to the Buda side of the city. Everything on the menu, including the drinks and cocktails, taste good in this funky street art bar. A quieter alternative is available next door in the *Hadik* coffeehouse. *Daily | XI | Bartók Béla út 36–38 | www.szatyorbar.com | tram 18, 19, 41, 47, 49 Gárdonyi tér*

RESTAURANTS: EXPENSIVE

One special feature of the capital is its temples of Hungarian cuisine with breathtakingly beautiful décor. They include the *Kárpátia* (125 D3)(𝔐 D10) *(daily | V | Ferenciek tere 7–8 | tel. 1 3 17 35 96 | www.karpatia.hu)* and the *Mallhias Cellar (Mátyás Pince)* (125 D4) (𝔐 D10) *(daily | V | Március 15. tér 7 | at the Pest end of Elisabeth Bridge | tel. 1 26 68 0 08 | www. matyaspince.eu)* with its outstanding roma band. These addresses are a

★ **New York Kávéház**
Legendary and breathtakingly opulent → p. 59

★ **Costes Downtown**
Stylish, Michelin-starred restaurant with a bistro atmosphere → p. 60

★ **Csalogány 26**
The food is excellent, the atmosphere casual → p. 61

★ **Dobrumba**
An eclectic mix of Europe, Asia and Middle East on a plate → p. 62

★ **Napfényes étterem**
Huge portions of tasty vegan food served here → p. 65

MARCO POLO HIGHLIGHTS

visual treat, but be aware that they are also the preferred destinations of travel groups and tourists.

CAFÉ PIERROT (126 C2) (🗺 A8)

Do you appreciate fine food but are turned off by food snobs? Then head to Pierrot where even the simplest goulash soup tastes extraordinary. Other more refined dishes such as truffles or scallops will leave a lasting impression on your taste buds. The food somehow tastes even better served in the restaurant's "secret courtyard garden". *Daily |*

I | Fortuna utca 14 | tel. 1 3 75 69 71 | www.pierrot.hu | bus 16, 16A, 116

COSTES DOWNTOWN ⭐ (127 F3) (🗺 C9)

Michelin-star cuisine in a casual setting? Yes really! The motto here is fine dining in a bistro style atmosphere. Breakfast, lunch and dinner are all prepared in the open-plan kitchen and served to guests sat among contemporary works of art. This restaurant is a spin-off of Costes in the Ráday utca – the first Budapest restaurant to be awarded a Michelin star.

FAVOURITE EATERIES

Street food in the party district

Looking to grab a filling bite to eat? Then head to *Street Food Karaván* **(125 F2) (🗺 E9)** *(daily | VII | Kazinczy utca 18 | www.streetfoodkaravan.hu | metro 2:Astoria | Budget),* an outdoor food court with white pebbles and long benches which houses a dozen food trucks selling a variety of appetizing snacks from *lángos, kürtőskalács* and hamburgers to craft beer and homemade lemonade. A great, friendly place.

An authentic Budapest experience

Sometimes all you need are a few red and white chequered tablecloths, a great deal of hospitality and hearty portions of classic Hungarian food. The INSIDER TIP *Pozsonyi Kisvendéglő* **(131 D2) (🗺 D6)** *(daily | XIII | Radnóti Miklós utca 38 | tel. 1 7 87 48 77 | tram 2, 4, 6 Jászai Mari tér | Budget)* is an institution in Budapest attracting both locals and tourists to dine here. By the way, the Jókai bean soup is the perfect remedy for a hangover.

Books and films on the menu

The *KönyvBár* **(125 F1) (🗺 E9)** *(Closed Sun | VII | Dob utca 45 | tel. 20 9 22 70 27 | www.konyvbar.hu | tram 4, 6 Király utca | Moderate)* serves everything from Margaret Atwood's "The Handmaid's Tale", J.R.R. Tolkien's "Lord of the Rings" to Harry Potter. The restaurant is inspired to create dishes based on popular books and films, serving international cuisine in a bright and casual setting. A must for fans of literature and cinema.

Pool terrace

How does the idea of a glass of wine served in a children's swimming pool sound to you? Crazy? The disused pools, which once belonged to the Gellért baths, have been transformed into the outdoor gastropub *Pagony* **(135 D3) (🗺 D12)** *(daily | XI | Kememes utca 10 | tel. 31 7 83 64 11 | www.pagonykert.hu | metro 4: Szent Gellért tér | tram 19, 41, 47, 48, 49, 56 | Budget)* The empty pools are strangely atmospheric and the pub serves great food and drinks.

Michelin-star bistro or nouvelle cuisine? A stylish yet relaxed ambience in Costes Downtown

Daily | V | Vigyázó Ferenc utca 5 | tel. 1 9 20 10 15 | www.costesdowntown.hu | tram 2

CSALOGÁNY 26 ⭐
(130 B4) (*ØJ B7*)
Everything here is right: the Franco-Hungarian cuisine, the service and the relaxed atmosphere. You can enjoy the delicious dinners, but also a lunch menu for around 1,100 Ft. *Closed Sun, Mon | I | Csalogány utca 26 | tel. 1 2 0178 92 | www.csalogany26.hu | metro 2: Batthyány tér*

INSIDER TIP DÉRYNÉ BISZTRÓ
(126 C5) (*ØJ A9*)
This bistro takes good food, service and design seriously without being too snobbish. The menu is discrete but everything is prepared to perfection and there is a great ● served on Sundays between 9am and 4pm. By the way, the cosy cabin in front of the restaurant is used for baking the deliciously homemade Déryné bread. Try it for yourself. *Daily | I | Krisztina tér 3 | tel. 1 2 25 14 07 | www.bistroderyne.com | tram 17, 19, 41, 56 | bus 105*

ÉS BISZTRÓ (125 D2) (*ØJ D9*)
In Hungarian, és means "and" and true to its word this bistro is a steakhouse and luxury restaurant, pub and wine bar combining a relaxing atmosphere and extremely high quality all in one. Order the hay steak if you want the ultimate steak experience – Austrian beef which has been wrapped in hay and herbs and stored for three weeks. A pleasure for all the senses. *Daily | V | Deák Ferenc utca 12–14 | tel. 1 4 29 39 90 | www.esbisztro.hu | metro 1, 2, 3: Deák Ferenc tér | tram 47, 48, 49*

LOCAL SPECIALITIES

barackos gombóc – dumplings made of potato dough, stuffed with an apricot
Dobos-torta – famous cake made of six sponge layers, chocolate butter cream and a caramel glaze (photo right)
gesztenyepüré – chestnut dessert
gulyásleves – goulash soup)
Gundel-palacsinta – palacsinta (pancake) with filling (walnuts, candied orange peel, raisins and rum) and a chocolate sauce
halászlé – fish soup, typically consisting of several types of fish, such as carp, catfish and cod (photo left)
Hortobágyi palacsinta – palacsinta with a filling made chicken breast mince, sour cream, onions, peppers and tomatoes
lángos – deep fried flat bread made with a yeast-potato dough, served with a variety of fillings

lecsó – vegetable dish made of tomatoes, peppers and onions, served as a side or a stew
paprikás csirke – chicken, fried with onions, garlic and paprika and served with a sour cream sauce
rántott – breaded dishes (meat or fish). There are also battered vegetables, mostly served as a starter, such as *rántott karfiol* (cauliflower) or *rántott gombafejek* (mushrooms)
töltött káposzta – Hungarian stuffed cabbage. Further typical *töltött*-dishes are: stuffed onions *(töltött hagyma)* and peppers *(töltött paprika)*
túrós rétes – curd cheese strudel, served in many sweet and savoury variations
vörösboros meggyleves – popular fruit soup, the "tipsy morello cherry soup"

RESTAURANTS: MODERATE

DOBRUMBA ⭐ (125 E2) *(Ø E9)*
The Dobrumba restaurant is what Budapest has been waiting for: this hip establishment is geared to young people serving a delicious blend of flavours somewhere between Middle Eastern and Mediterranean cuisine. Fans of couscous and lamb come on in! Reservation is essential (open between 12 noon and 8pm). *Daily | VII | Dob Utca 5 | tel. 30 1 94 00 49 | www.dobrumba.hu | metro 2: Astoria | tram 47, 48, 49*

FAUSTO'S (125 E2) (*E10*)

This excellent restaurant, right next to the synagogue in Dohány utca, is relied upon for serving good Mediterranean cuisine. Its owner Fausto di Vora has been gastronomically active in Budapest for more than 20 years. He now offers a more formal restaurant and a more relaxed Osteria. *Closed Sun | VII | Dohány utca 3–5 | tel. 1 26 96 80 06 | www.osteria. hu | metro 2: Astoria | tram 47, 49*

HUNGARIKUM BISZTRÓ
(131 D4) (*C8*)

Situated in a quiet side street in Leopold town, this friendly restaurant strives to put traditional Hungarian cuisine back on the map. Furnished in rustic country-inn style, it specialises in culinary meat dishes typical of Hungary. Sweet pancakes are the obvious choice for desert. Reservation essential! *Daily | V | Steindl Imre utca 13 | tel. 1 79 77 17 77 and 30 6 61 62 44 | www.hungarikumbisztro.hu | metro 2: Kossuth Lajos tér | tram 2*

KŐLEVES VENDÉGLŐ (125 E1) (*E9*)

A glance at the restaurant's website reveals the vibe of the Köleves: The basic ingredients – pasta, bread, jams and sauces – are homemade and all the dishes are made with seasonal produce. The INSIDER TIP atmospheric outdoor beer garden next door (open only in summer) also serves barbecued food. Located in the centre of the Jewish Quarter, the restaurant itself is housed in the building of an old kosher meat plant – and in keeping with tradition, there are no pork dishes on the menu. *Daily | VII | Kazinczy utca 41 | tel. 20 2 13 59 99 | www.kolevesvendeglo.hu | metro 2: Astoria | tram 47, 48, 49*

STÉG (125 E1) (*E9*)

Do you have a weakness for fish? Or just fancy a bowl of *halászlé* (fish soup)?

Then Stég is the ideal place – a small, tastefully decorated restaurant serving classics such as fish and chips. However the best is to try the *keszeg*, a type of carp and Hungarian specialty with one of the excellent Hungarian wines from the wine presses Sauska and Dúzsi Tamás. The restaurant also serves *lángos*

Hearty specialty: a bowl of goulash soup

if there are any vegetarians among you. A set meal is served every weekday. *Daily | VII | in Gozsdu Court | Dob utca 16 | tel. 1 8 78 13 28 | www.stcgfood.hu | metro 1, 2, 3: Deák Ferenc tér | tram 47, 48, 49*

VÖRÖS POSTAKOCSI (125 F5) (*E11*)

Those who wish to experience Hungarian cuisine along with a Hungarian atmosphere should try the "Red Stagecoach". You can sample meat from mangalica pigs and grey cattle, and there's music and folklore in the evenings. Beer and meat lovers will want to go to the *Beer Cellar*. Alongside a large choice of beers, they have steaks from Argentinean Angus cattle. Large terrace during the summer. *Daily | IX | Ráday utca 15 | tel.*

1 2 17 67 56 | www.vorospk.com | metro 3, 4: Kálvin tér

RESTAURANTS: BUDGET

INSIDER TIP ▶ BORS GASZTRÓBÁR
(125 F2) *(⌘ E9)*

In Hungary, the saying is "The pepper is small yet spicy" meaning roughly the equivalent of "small things come in small packages" and it is a fitting description for this street food bar come bistro. The chefs György Rethling and Tamás Lipher create soups to go (sic!), gourmet grilled baguettes, pasta dishes with a twist plus delicious juices and desserts. Judging by the interior design and background music, they obviously share a passion for Star Wars and rap music. A tiny yet delightful establishment. *Closed Sun | VII | Kazinczy utca 10 | tel. 70 9 35 32 63 | borsgasztroweb.wixsite.com/ bors-gasztrobar | metro 2: Astoria | tram 47, 49*

FRUCCOLA
(124 C2) *(⌘ D10)*

Fresh fruit juices and salads, crunchy croissants for breakfast and cheap lunches – the Fruccola is a contrast to Hungarian food, which can be heavy sometimes. You can put together your own salad and there is a choice of daily meals and desserts. Ideal for vegetarians and vegans. *Closed Sun | V | Kristóf tér 3 | metro 1: Vörösmarty tér; branch:* **(131 D–E5)** *(⌘ D8) (V | Arany János utca 32 | metro 3: Arany János tér); tel. 1 4 30 61 25 | www.fruccola.hu*

GERLÓCZY
(125 D2) *(⌘ D10)*

A touch of Paris in Budapest – the Gerlóczy is a friendly café restaurant with a wonderful terrace in a small square in the city centre. Breakfast is worth the walk and in the evenings you can dine pleasantly under colourful lanterns. You can rent comfortable rooms on the upper floors. *Daily | V | Gerlóczy utca 1 | tel. 1 5 01 40 00 | www.gerloczy.hu | metro 2: Astoria | tram 47, 49*

HUMMUS BAR **(125 E4)** *(⌘ E10)*

You like falafel and hummus? Then you're well looked after in the brnaches of the Hummus Bar. Also takeaway. Especially tasty: the shakshuka! Several branches. *Daily | VI | Nagymező utca 10 | tel. 20 3 99 00 37 | metro 1: Opera; branch:* **(131 D5)** *(⌘ D8) (V | Október 6. utca 19 | tel. 1 3 54 01 08 | metro 3: Arany János utca); www.hummusbar.hu*

LOW BUDGET

In the ● *Central Market Hall* **(135 E2)** *(⌘ D–E11) (IX | Vámház körút 1–3 | tram 2, 47, 49)* on the 1st floor you can buy savoury or sweet *langós* for 620 Ft. (flat bread made from a yeast-potato dough with, for example, sour cream and cheese) – delicious! The price is for a basic langós; extras will cost more.

Only a stone's throw from Liszt Ferenc tér *Napos Oldal* **(131 F4)** *(⌘ E8) (closed Sun | VI | Jókai utca 7–8 | metro 1: Oktogon)* offers vegetarian snacks and cakes for 300–1,200 Ft.

There are many vegetable dishes (620–1,200 Ft.) to choose from in *Főzelékfaló* **(131 E4)** *(⌘ E8) (closed Sun | VI | Nagymező utca 18 | no tel. | metro 1: Opera)*. Meat dishes, soups, salads and sweet treats too.

MENZA (129 F4) (*M E8*)

Decorated in a trendy 70s and 80s style. The menu lists many soups and salads as well as main dishes ranging from penne to *lángos* and duck. The palacsinta with quark covered in vanilla sauce and meringue is delicious. Inexpensive daily specials. *Daily | VI | Liszt Ferenc tér 2 | tel. 1 4 13 14 82 | www.menzaetterem. hu | metro 1: Oktogon*

NAPFÉNYES ÉTTEREM ★
(125 D3) (*M D10*)

Napfény translates as sunshine, a perfect word to sum up this vegan restaurant in meat-loving Budapest. The enormous portions are enough to fill the most passionate carnivores. The delicious food ranges from Hungarian to international and you can put together your own salads at the salad bar. There is also a set meal served every weekday. No alcoholic or caffeine beverages are served. *Daily | V | Ferenciek tere 2 | tel. 20 3 11 03 13 | www.napfenyesetterem.hu*

INSIDER TIP ORIENTAL SOUP HOUSE
(131 D2) (*M D6*)

Budapest is awash with Asian and especially Chinese restaurants – but beware many are not authentic. On the other hand, the Oriental Soup House serves genuine Asian dishes such as pho and dim sums in hearty portions. Both the service and interior design are also appealing. Good vegetarian and vegan options available. *Daily | XII | Balzac utca 35 | tel. 70 6 17 35 35 | www. facebook.com/orientalsouphouse | tram 4, 6 Jászai Mari tér*

SPINOZA (125 E2) (*M E9*)

In the heart of the old Jewish quarter is the Spinoza – a successful crossover of simple restaurant, stylish café and event place for Klezmer evenings (Fridays from 7pm). Evenings are regularly accompanied by piano music. *Daily | VII | Dob utca 15 | tel. 1 4 12 74 88 | www. spinozahaz.hu | metro 2: Astoria | tram 47, 48, 49*

Retro-style restaurant: Menza on the trendy square at Liszt Ferenc tér

SHOPPING

CITY **WHERE TO START?**
Váci utca (124–125 C–D2–5)
(🔲 D9–10) and its side streets are a shopping Mecca. International fashion and shoe labels are represented here, as are small Hungarian shops. Vörösmarty tér is home to new shopping centres, if you turn right you will find yourself in the small Deák Ferenc utca ("Fashion Street"). Looking for international luxury brands? Then explore the boulevard **Andrássy út (131 E–F 4–5, 132 A–B 2–4)** *(🔲 D–F 7–9)*. The largest shopping centre is the **Westend City Center (131 E2–3)** *(🔲 D–E 6–7)*.

Good news for everyone mad about shopping and hunting for souvenirs: **Shopping is as much part of Budapest culture as its coffeehouses. Run-of-the-mill chain stores, out-of-the-ordinary art shops or markets – the choice is entirely up to you.**

The pedestrian zone Váci utca in Pest is packed with shops selling everything from international and Hungarian fashion and beauty brands to porcelain, folklore and classic kitschy souvenirs. The southern section (Szabad sajtó út to Fővám tér) is quieter and you will find smaller shops with Hungarian products. Király utca, which runs parallel to Andrássy út, is a top address for design fans with its furniture and home furnishings shops. The 4.5-km (3-mile) Grand

Whether it's culinary treats, glass and porcelain or fashion and young designs: you can get almost anything in Budapest

Boulevard (Nagykörút) between Margaret Bridge and Petőfi Bridge still has nostalgic shops (selling, for example, fabrics), which are, however, gradually disappearing. The young in particular are drawn to shopping centres with their ranges of fashion outlets, restaurants and cinemas.

Hungarian specialties are always a popular souvenir, the most edible of which include the spicy Hungarian salami or smoked sausage *(szalámi, kolbász)*, marzipan (e.g., from Szamos), wine *(bor)*,

fruit brandy *(pálinka)* and herbal liqueur *(unicum)*. Other favourites to take back home are ceramics and porcelain (Zsolnay, Herend) and hand-embroidered tablecloths (especially those in Matyó style). Young designers are reinventing traditional patterns, for example those on display in the Fian Koncept store (see page 71). Casual streetwear like the items on sale in the BP Shop (see page 71) are also popular and the t-shirts with the inscription "Buda fckn Pest" are worn with pride by young Hungarians and

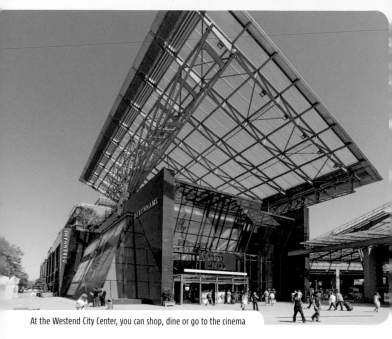

At the Westend City Center, you can shop, dine or go to the cinema

tourists alike. The Falk Miksa utca is known as Budapest's antique row and is lined with renowned antique shops and art galleries.

ANTIQUES & GALLERIES

NAGYHÁZI (131 D3) (*ω C7*)
Jewellery, antique furniture, carpets, porcelain, paintings and more: this family-owned auction house is always worth a visit. Often discount campaigns. *V | Balaton utca 8 | corner of Falk Miksa utca | www.nagyhazi.hu | tram 2, 4, 6*

INSIDER TIP TABÁNI GARÁZSVÁSÁR (124 B3) (*ω C10*)
It's no coincidence that this antique store is known as a "garage sale": Unlike the other more high-end antique dealers on the Falk Miksa utca, Zsolt

Rédei`s store is lined with shelves full of bric-a-brac. Maci is the name of the owner's cute dog that usually lies sprawled out in the entrance – just climb over him! *I | Döbrentei utca 10 | tram 19, 41 Várkert Bazár*

BOOKS & MUSIC

MASSOLIT BOOKS & CAFÉ (125 F1–2) (*ω E9*)
Coffee, cakes and snacks but above all books are available in this endearing cultural café which you'll fall in love with as soon as you enter. The foreign-language books are aimed at an open and tolerant crowd with themes such as progressive politics, feminism and Jewish studies rather than mainstream literature. There's a INSIDER TIP cosy, shady garden and there are frquent public read-

ings, film clubs and acoustic concerts. *VII | Nagy Diófa utca 30 | www.facebook. com/MassolitBudapest | metro 2: Blaha Lujza tér*

ROCKIN' BOX (125 D1) (*山 D9*)
On the front it says in big letters "rockabilly, beat, country, rock 'n' roll, blues" and this quirky second-hand record store has a great selection of well assorted vinyls, popular not only with fans of oldies. The walls are decorated with album covers and retro guitars and the 1st floor houses a collection of old radios. Make sure to visit before it is turned into a hip café. *VI | Paulay Ede utca 8 | metro 1: Bajcsy-Zsilinszky út*

SHOPPING & LEISURE CENTRES

MOM PARK (134 A2) (*山 A10*)
Modern shopping centre which attracts a posher crowd of Buda locals with cash-filled wallets. The lower level has some great delicatessens; amongst them is the Bortársaság wine store. *XII | Alkotás út 53/corner of Csörsz utca | www.mompark. hu | tram 61*

WESTEND CITY CENTER ⭐
(123 E2–3) (*山 D–E 6–7*)
This bright temple of consumerism has countless shops from fashion to technics. There are touchscreens dotted around the centre providing information on where visitors are currently located. The lower floor is a food court hall serving all types of fast food (the delicious Indian-Pakistani *Kohinoor* is particularly recommended) and the top floor houses *Cinema City* where English-language films are often showing. The rooftop terrace also has an ice rink in winter. *VI | Váci út 1–3 | near Western Station | www.westend. hu | metro 3: Nyugati pályaudvar*

FOLKLORE

KAROLINA GALÉRIA (132 A4) (*山 E8*)
Here you can watch the potter at work and even take samples home with you. Inconspicuous from the outside, the store specialises in ceramics that are lovingly painted by hand. The only problem is what to choose – Budapest cups, cat wall clocks, Christmas tree decorations and the list goes on and on! *VI | Andrássy út 55 | www. karolinagaleria.hu | tram 4, 6 Oktogon*

NÉPMŰVÉSZETI BOLT ⭐
(125 D3) (*山 D10*)
Whether carved, embroidered or painted, this "folklore store" in the city centre sells a stunning collection of Hungarian arts and crafts made of wood, fabrics and ceramic. *V | Régiposta utca 12 | www.*

⭐ **Westend City Center**
Budapest's largest shopping centre → **p. 69**

⭐ **Népművészeti Bolt**
Hungarian handicrafts in the heart of the city → **p. 69**

⭐ **Central Market Hall**
Paprika and salami under steel and glass → **p. 71**

⭐ **Nanushka**
Young, minimalistic and extremely stylish → **p. 72**

⭐ **Herend Porcelain**
Hungary's finest porcelain → **p. 72**

⭐ **Bortársaság**
Amazing selection of Hungarian wines → **p. 73**

MARCO POLO HIGHLIGHTS

folkartkezmuveshaz.hu | metro 1: Vörösmarty tér

MARKETS & DELICACIES

INSIDER TIP **CULINARIS** (131 D3) (*C7*)

This delicatessen sells delicacies from all over the world. If you wanted a picnic, for example, you could get fine antipasti, rolls, cheese and wine here. *V | Balassi Bálint utca 7 | tram 2, 4, 6; branch:* (128 A3) (*C3*) *(III | Perc utca 8 | bus 9 Tímár utca); www.culinaris.hu*

FÉNY UTCAI PIAC (130 A3) (*A7*)

The market along the Fény utca is worth visiting for its authentic Hungarian market atmosphere and delicious specialties. Here, friendly old ladies sell vegetables grown in their own gardens. You will also find the traditional Mangalica smoked sausage and the *lángos* stall on the first floor is legendary (even if its appearance is nothing to go by). The market stalls usually open at 6am and close around 2pm. *II | Lövőház utca 12 | tram 4, 6 Széna tér*

INSIDER TIP **WAMP DESIGN MARKET** (125 D1) (*D9*)

Young Hungarian designers, market atmosphere, earrings upcycled from buttons and bags from rubber bike tyres, hand-painted crockery and hand-sewn ties – the list is never ending... The market is unique, specialising in DIY and upcycled products. It is usually held the first Sunday of the month from April to September on the Erzsébet tér and otherwise indoor in the Millenáris cultural and recreational centre *V | Erzsébet tér | at the metro station Deák Ferenc tér; Millenáris:* (130 A3) (*A7*) *(II | Kis Rókus utca 16–20 | tram 4, 6 Széna tér); www.wamp.hu/en*

Not exactly the easiest souvenir to transport – how about garlic or Hungarian pepper instead?

CENTRAL MARKET HALL (KÖZPONTI VÁSÁRCSARNOK) ★ ●
(135 E2) (*∅ D–E11*)

You will get the best view of the 150-m (492 ft) long market hall with its two aisles from one of the transverse corridors on the top floor. Designed by Samu Pecz, this beautiful building was extremely modern at the time it was built in the 1890s. Even though almost no visitor to Budapest leaves without seeing it, it is not an establishment for tourists, but one of the country's most important markets. Whether it's fruit, vegetables, meat or fish: this place sells everything the heart desires. If you're looking for souvenirs, you can buy them on the first floor. Haggle! *IX | Vámház körút 1–3 | metro 4: Fővám tér | tram 2, 47, 49*

FASHION & DESIGN

BP SHOP (125 E2) (*∅ E9*)

The cool young guys behind the fashion label BP are so proud of their home city, they print it large on their ultra-casual, hip-hop style t-shirts, caps, hoodies and shoes. New collections for both men and women on a regular basis – perfect as a cool souvenir! *VI | Wesselényi utca 24 | www.bpshop.hu | metro 2: Blaha Lujza tér*

DEÁK FERENC UTCA
(124–125 C–D2) (*∅ D9*)

This road is also known as "Fashion Street" because a large number of clothing brands have opened shops here, such as Hugo Boss, Prada, Tommy Hilfiger and Dolce & Gabbana. *V | Deák Ferenc utca | metro 1, 2, 3: Deák Ferenc tér*

ÉKES KESZTYŰ (125 D3) (*∅ D10*)

This small, unassuming shop in the city centre in Pest sells handmade gloves and hats manufactured by a local family in its third generation (*ékes kesztyű* = pretty glove). *V | Régiposta utca 14 | metro 1: Vörösmarty tér*

FIAN KONCEPT (126 B2) (*∅ A8*)

This store is a paradise for shoppers – and beware there are two of them in Budapest. Both branches are located on the Buda side of the city in the castle district and you'll have no difficulty spending your money on Hungarian fashion, accessories and gift items. The most exciting labels are Romani Design from the Romani Varga sisters and Piroshka by the German-Hungarian fashion designer Anna Hegedűs – both labels combine traditional patterns and fabrics with today's fashion. *I | Úri utca 26–28 and Fortuna utca 18 | www.fian.hu | bus 16, 16A, 116*

INSIDER TIP ▶ HUMANA VINTAGE BUTIK
(135 E1) (*∅ E10*)

Looking for something out of the ordinary rather than off-the-peg but don't want to trek around the shops? Whatever your style, this compact vintage spinoff store from the Humana chain of second-hand shops is for you. Expect to be asked back home though where you got your amazing clothes from. *V | Károly körút 8 | www.humanahasznaltruha.hu/vintagebutik.html | metro 2: Astoria | tram 47, 49*

INSITU (125 E3) (*∅ E10*)

An incredible shop! Clothes and accessories of Hungarian brands such as Balkantango, top-class electronic gadgets such as fish-eye cameras, fun jewellery made of plastic insects, colourful wristwatches and, upstairs, a storeroom where it's okay to rummage around. *V | Múzeum körút 7 | in the passage | www.insitu.hu | metro 2: Astoria*

INSIDERTIP MONOFASHION SHOP
(125 E3) (*D10*)

Mono was one of the first stores in Budapest to sell fashion designed by young Hungarians. The choice is amazing (even for men) and is continuously updated; there is something affordable for everyone's wallet. The store also has an interesting collection of jewellery and accessory items. *V | Kossuth Lajos utca 20 | www.facebook.com/monofashion | metro 2: Astoria | tram 47, 48, 49*

NANUSHKA ⭐ (124 C2) (*J1*)

"Nanuska" was the nickname of fashion designer Szandra Sándor when she was a young girl. Nobody would of thought back then that she would go on to create her own fashion label sold in stores from New York to Hong Kong. Her designs are up-to-the-minute yet timeless, playful and minimalistic. *V | Bécsi utca 3 | www.nanushka.com | metro 1: Vörösmarty tér*

PRINTA 🌐 (131 E6) (*E9*)

A creative centre for environmentally-conscious design, exhibitions, art and textile prints. You can buy clothes such as T-shirts, as well as bags, lampshades and jewellery from 17 different designers. The coffee available in the café comes from a fair trade project. *VII | Rumbach Sebestyén utca 10 | www.printa.hu | metro 1, 2, 3: Deák Ferenc tér*

RETROCK (125 D1) (*D9*)

Only a few meters from the junction Deák Ferenc tér in a side-street is this hip store for clothes, attracting the young people of Budapest. The handbags and shoes are cool as well. On the Egyetem tér is the somewhat upper-class branch *Retrock de Luxe* with creations of young Hungarian designers. *VI | Anker köz 2 | metro 1, 2, 3: Deák Ferenc tér; Retrock de Luxe: (125 E4)(* *E10*) *(V | Henszlmann Imre utca 1 | metro 3, 4: Kálvin tér); www.retrock.com*

LOW BUDGET

Lovers of crystal and handicrafts such as embroidered pieces (e.g. tablecloths) will find these can still be bought quite cheaply in Budapest , e.g. crystal at *Ajka Kristály*, embroidery in the *Népművészeti Bolt*.

Fresh fruit and vegetables as well as other groceries can be bought at reasonable prices in old city quarter market halls. The largest and nicest one is situated at the metro station Rákóczi tér on the Large Central Ring **(136 B1)** (*F10*).

PORCELAIN, POTTERY & GLASS

AJKA KRISTÁLY (125 E3) (*D10*)

You think Bohemia crystal is special? Then check out the magnificent glass art originating from Ajka in the west of Hungary which is easily on a par with the legendary crystal. The glassware is hand-cut, finely engraved and surprisingly understated in design. The store's antique interior design is also special with its delightful wood carvings. Don't be put off by the shop's unappealing exterior. *V | Kossuth Lajos utca 10 | www.ajka-crystal.hu | metro 2: Astoria | tram 47, 48, 49*

HEREND PORCELAIN ⭐
(124 C1) (*D8*)

You could be fooled into thinking that porcelain is boring and only for older people. You'd be wrong! Visit a shop selling Herend porcelain. This vintage brand is world-famous and has managed to preserve its tradition for almost 200 years. Many of the contemporary designs are on a par with the porcelain craftsmanship from the past. (126 C3) *(🛒 B9) (I | Szentháromság utca 5 | bus 16, 16A, 116);* (124 C3) *(🛒 D9) (V | József Nádor tér 11 | metro 1: Vörösmarty tér);* (131 E5) *(🛒 D8) (VI | Andrássy út 16 | metro 1: Opera); www.herend.com*

ZSOLNAY (125 E4) *(🛒 E10)*

The porcelain manufacture based in the Southern Hungarian city of Pécs not only achieved fame with its colourful tiles that decorate many of Budapest's magnificent Wilhelminian-style buildings dating back to the industrial revolution. The company is also synonymous with Art Nouveau in Hungary. *V | Kálvin tér 1/corner of Kecskeméti utca | metro 3, 4: Kálvin tér*

TISZA CIPŐ (125 E2) *(🛒 E10)*

This Communist era brand has managed to achieve cult status. Young Hungarians are discovering these shoes with the stylized "T" as a cool alternative to conventional labels. Also womens' and mens' sportswear, bags and rucksacks. There's also a branch at the Westend City Center, but the Astoria store is nicer. *VII | Károly körút 1 | www.tiszacipo.hu | metro 2: Astoria | tram 47, 48, 49*

VASS (125 D3) *(🛒 D10)*

Vass is an institution! The hand-made shoes from this traditional workshop are equal to any made-to-measure items from London. The shop sells ready-to-wear shoes for men and women, or you can have your measurements taken for your own last. *V | Haris köz 6 | www.vass-cipo.hu | metro 3: Ferenciek tere*

BORTÁRSASÁG ⭐ (131 D4) *(🛒 C8)*

Hungary is an excellent wine region, from the sundrenched wine regions in the south at Villány, Pécs and Szekszárd right up to the famous wine regions Tokaj and Eger in the north. The wine trading company Bortársaság, among other things, operates its own, well assorted wine shop. *V | Vécsey utca 5 | corner of Vértanúk tere | www.bortarsasag.hu | metro 2: Kossuth Lajos tér | tram 2*

PÁLINKA HOUSE (125 F2) *(🛒 E10)*

Hungarian fruit brandies *(pálinka)* have won several awards at the top European fair, the Destillata in Austria. Products from the top distilleries can be found here. *VIII | Rákóczi út 17 | www.magyar palinkahaza.hu | metro 2: Astoria | tram 47, 49*

Perfect craftsmanship by Vass

ENTERTAINMENT

CITY WHERE TO START?

An evening out in Budapest is best spent in the **Jewish Quarter (131 E–F 5–6)** *(ꬉ D–E9)*, also known as the party district *(bulinegyed)*. The more alternative hot spots around Madách Imre tér and in the Gozsdu Court offer something for everyone. Budapest is famous for its ruin pubs and the colourful Szimpla kert is arguably the top-choice xperience. On warm summer evenings, city dwellers gather along the **Danube** – music fans love the concert ship *A38* **(135 F4)** *(ꬉ E13)* on the Buda side.

There is no doubt that you can party the night away in Budapest whether on a party boat, rooftop terrace or in a ruin pub. But away from the vibrant clubbing scene, the city has even more to offer.

"Budapest by night" may sound like a phrase from a cheesy postcard but the city does have an unmistakably magical charm in the evenings which attracts the many locals to head to the pubs and clubs or take a stroll after sunset. What's for sure: If you're not into partying and loud nightlife isn't your scene, you should probably avoid the Jewish Quarter and Nagymezö utca, the street at the heart of the city's party district. But of course the city has enough alternatives to choose from.

Forays through Budapest's nightlife: operas, concerts and operettas are no less outstanding than the city's pubs and clubs

The people of Budapest love going to the theatre, but for tourists there is the language barrier to contend with. For that reason a visit to the opera is a must, for the fantastic ambience alone. Musicals have their firm place and the good old operetta has also been able to assert itself successfully in the home of Franz Léhar and Imre Kálmán. Information on events from techno parties to opera can be found on *www.welovebudapest.com*.

BARS & PUBS

ANKER'T (131 E5) (*⫴ E8*)

Large, party covered location which serves as a beer garden in the evening, throbbing club at night and a vegan market on Sundays. It attracts a diverse crowd from locals to expats and tourists. Everyone is welcome, including children and dogs. The food bar serves fast-food burgers, quesadillas and salads. *Daily 3pm–3am | VI | Paulay Ede utca 33 | www. facebook.com/ankertbar | metro 1: Opera*

Fans of Budapest's "ruin pubs" have come to the right place – the Szimpla Kert beer garden

INSIDER TIP BAMBI ESZPRESSZÓ (130 C3) (*ØØ B7*)

With its red leather furniture, white lace tablecloths and yellow retro mosaics, time seems to have stood still in Bambi since it opened in the 1960s and yet this popular restaurant has retained its charm. Even the menu throws up old classics such as *melegszendvics* (a slice of white bread with melted cheese and ketchup), debrecener sausages, cakes, coffee, beer and fruit syrups. You can sit outside or inside among the old men playing traditional board games – here you can still experience the authentic *preszó* genre. *Mon–Fri 7am–10pm, Sat/Sun 9am–10pm | II | Frankel Leó utca 2–4 | www.facebook.com/bambieszpresszo | tram 4, 6 Margit híd, budai hídfő*

CSENDES LÉTTEREM (125 E3) (*ØØ E10*)

The Csendes chain has spread across Budapest, with not just one but four attractive locations. The Létterem was the first of its kind – a relaxed, creatively decorated bar whose main clientele are students from the elite university nearby. Snacks and breakfast are also on sale. *Csendes Társ, Csendes – A Pesti Szatócs* and the ✪ vegan bistro *Csendes M* are all just a stone's throw away near Károlyi Kert. *Mon–Thu from noon, Fri from 2pm, Sat from 4pm | V | Ferenczy István utca 7 | www.csend.es | metro 2: Astoria | tram 47, 48, 49*

DIVINO WINE BAR

Hungarian wine is massively underrated, don't you think? If you haven't tasted any yet, try a glass at the Divino wine bar.

And don't worry if you can't taste the difference between a Sauvignon Blanc and Franc – the extremely polite and professional waiters are on hand to help. The bar also serves accompanying dishes from cheese to pork ribs; the Hungarian mixed platter is particularly recommended. Relaxed atmosphere in an exclusive setting. *Bazilika:* (131 E5) *(Ø D9)* V | *Szent István tér 3 | metro 1: Bajcsy-Zsilinszky út; Gozsdu:* (125 E1) *(Ø E9)* VII | *Király utca 13 | metro 1, 2, 3: Deák Ferenc tér | tram 47, 48, 49*

INSIDERTIP ÉLESZTŐHÁZ
(136 A3) *(Ø F11)*

You can order any drink you like.... as long as it's beer! Those who can't get enough of the malt beverage will feel at home here sitting either in the shady courtyard or the spacious interior decorated with open red brick walls and contemporary wooden furniture. They serve mainly Hungarian craft beers and ales – try for example the tasty mint chocolate stout brewed by the Szent András brewery. *The Vino-Piano Wein & Tapas Bar* next door makes sure you don't starve after the generous beer consumption. *Daily 3pm–3am | IX | Tűzoltó utca 22 | www.elesztohaz.hu | metro 3: Corvin-negyed | tram 3, 4*

MIKA TIVADAR MULATÓ
(125 E1) *(Ø E9)*

Mulató is a nostalgic word literally meaning a place of entertainment and is a fitting description for the Mika pub. Inside, wooden tables and chairs are set out like in a coffeehouse with chandeliers hanging from the ceiling. The cellar is used for dancing or concerts. If things get too warm down there, cool down in the pub's outdoor seating area. *Daily from 4pm | VII | Kazinczy utca 47 | www.mikativadarmulato.hu | metro 1: Opera*

SZIMPLA KERT ★ ● (125 F2) *(Ø E9)*

Szimpla Kert was the first of Budapest's extremely hyped "ruin pubs" and attracts crowds of tourists and expats. Surrounded by crumbling walls, the courtyard garden is particularly popular in summer where you can also smoke shishas. It's worth taking a peek at all the wildly decorated rooms inside. *Daily from noon | VII | Kazinczy utca 14 | www.szimpla.hu | metro 2: Astoria | tram 47, 48, 49*

INSIDERTIP TELEP (125 E1) *(Ø E9)*

What started life as a small pub for skateboarders and the hip-hop scene has be-

---

MARCO POLO HIGHLIGHTS

★ **Szimpla kert**
Always something happening in Budapest's first ruin pub
→ p. 77

★ **Uránia**
Old-fashioned cinema and architectural gem → p. 78

★ **Béla Bartók Concert Hall**
The top address for classical concerts in the Palace of Arts
→ p. 78

★ **Liszt Ferenc Academy of Music**
A harmony of architecture and music → p. 79

★ **Opera**
Magnificent musical theatre with a look behind the scenes
→ p. 79

★ **Budapest Jazz Club**
Talented, international jazz musicians and fine-dining menu
→ p. 81

come an extremely popular hangout for trendy, young city dwellers. The cliché Telep visitor is a full-bearded, tattooed man with a dog. The *Központ* opposite belongs to the same proprietor and is similar in style. *Mon–Fri noon–2am, Sat 4pm–2am | VII | Madách Imre út 8 | www.facebook.com/telepgaleria |metro 1, 2, 3: Deák Ferenc tér | tram 47, 48, 49*

CINEMAS

MŰVÉSZ, PUSKIN, TOLDI
Budapest has an excellent selection of independent and art-house cinemas. We have chosen the three most authentic which show international films with Hungarian subtitles and provide English subtitles for Hungarian-spoken films. The Művész picture house with five screens is particularly worth visiting. The Toldi regularly organises great. INSIDER TIP partys and concerts. *Művész (131 E4)(ﬁ E8) (VI | Teréz körút 30 | metro 3: Nyugati pályaudvar); Puskin (125 E3) (ﬁ D10) (V | Kossuth Lajos utca 18 | metro 3: Ferenciek tere); Toldi*

LOW BUDGET

Cheap tickets are sold for the top 3rd gallery in the *Opera* or 5th category in the *Operetta Theatre* (with restricted views of the stage) and are available for 2–5 euros.

Opus Jazz Club: Just a few minutes on foot from the Kálvin tér is an insider tip for all jazz fans out there in the *Budapest Music Center*. The admission price (3–6 euros) is an absolute bargain and they are known to organise free concerts.

(131 E4) *(ﬁ D8) (V | Bajcsy-Zsilinszky út 36–38 | metro 3: Arany János utca); www.artmozi.hu*

URÁNIA ★ (132 A6) *(ﬁ F9)*
Believe it or not, the Uránia cinema has been showing documentary films for over 100 years – today it is also a venue for concerts, ballet performances, public readings and a coffee shop. The building is a stunning piece of architecture, both inside and out, combining Venetian Gothic, Italian Renaissance and Arabic-Moorish styles. In other words: don't miss it! *VII | Rákóczi út 25 | www.urania-nf.hu | metro 2: Blaha Lujza tér | bus 7*

CONCERTS, OPERAS & OPERETTAS

BÉLA BARTÓK CONCERT HALL (BARTÓK BÉLA NEMZETI HANGVERSENYTEREM) ★ ● (136 A6) *(ﬁ F14)*
The "National Béla Bartók Concert Hall", with its 1,700 seats is the core of the Palace of Arts. Its acoustics are a marvel of modern engineering. This concert hall sees performances by the Hungarian National Philharmonic Orchestra as well as major orchestras and soloists from around the world. *IX | Komor Marcell utca 1 | www.mupa.hu | tram 2, 24 Millenniumi Kulturális Központ*

BUDAPEST MUSIC CENTER (125 E6) *(ﬁ E11)*
The BMC is the dream come true for trombonist and music instructor László Gőz who founded the cultural and information centre with music database and library in 1996. Featuring a neoclassical façade and very contemporary interior, the building is an excellent piece of architecture. Sophisticated chamber music is played in the *Opus Jazz Club* and the concert hall is a popular venue for pop

and classical music. *IX | Mátyás utca 8 | Tel. 1 2 16 78 94 | www.bmc.hu | metro 3, 4: Kálvin tér | tram 47, 48, 49*

LISZT-FERENC ACADEMY OF MUSIC (ZENEAKADÉMIA) ⭐ (131 F4–5) *(ⓜ E8)*

A masterpiece from both inside and outside – the Franz Liszt Academy of Music is Hungary's most influential music school with an excellent international reputation and a great place to hear classical music often played by students from the academy. The façade of the building (completed in 1907 and extensively renovated in 2013) is mesmerizing and the foyer and large hall are splendid examples of Hungarian Art Nouveau. There is no need to pre-book; tickets are available at the box office. *No performances July/Aug | guided tours in English daily 1:30pm | VI | Liszt Ferenc tér 8 | tel. 14 62 46 00 | zeneakademia.hu/en | metro 1: Oktogon | tram 4, 6*

COMEDY THEATRE (VÍGSZÍNHÁZ) (131 D3) *(ⓜ D7)*

The theatre, opened in 1896, is a masterpiece of architectural eclecticism. Performances include classics such as William Shakespeare and Friedrich Dürrenmatt. There are also other good productions you can go and see for which you do not need to understand Hungarian, such as "The Jungle Book" or "The Wizard of Oz". *No performances June–Sept | XIII | Szent István körút 14 | tel. 1 3 40 46 50 | www.vigszinhaz.hu | tram 2, 4, 6 Jászai Mari tér*

OPERA (OPERAHÁZ) ⭐ (131 E5) *(ⓜ D–E8)*

The opera is renowned for showing great works of art from Italian operas, and international ballet performances to Hungarian classical concerts. Accompanying the great programme is the visual pleasure of the surroundings.

During an interval, standing on one of the balconies that look out on Andrássy út is a special experience. Performances sell out quickly, so check out the programme as early as you can. Tickets are available online or from the opera shop (at the side, in Hajós utca). *VI | Andrássy*

Hi-tech for sound: the Bélá Bartók Concert Hall

út 22 | tel. 1 3 32 79 14 | www.opera.hu | metro 1: Opera

OPERETTA THEATRE (OPERETT-SZÍNHÁZ) (131 E4) *(ⓜ E8)*

"Operetta" may sound slightly old-fashioned but this music theatre, situated on the "Budapest Broadway", puts on contemporary and intellectually demand-

Crossover on the Danube: the A38 club boat complete with restaurant and young music

ing pieces. Its repertoire includes "The Gypsy Princess" by Hungarian composer Emmerich Kálmán, "The Hunchback of Notre-Dame" and "Romeo and Juliet". The ideal place to see a performance is in the freshly renovated *Kálmán Imre Teátrum* auditorium. *VI | Nagymező utca 17 | tel. 1 35 32172 | www.operettszinhaz.hu | metro 1: Opera*

MUSIC CLUBS

INSIDER TIP ▶ **A38** (131 F5) (∅ F13)

Moored on the Buda side, the A38 is a decommissioned Ukrainian stone hauler and now the city's most popular live-music venue. There is a great restaurant on the upper deck while the ship's hull provides fantastic acoustics for live concerts. Tip: *Random Trip* is a series of concerts where young talented musicians from the Hungarian music scene perform. *Daily | XI | on the Buda side at the Petőfi bridge | www.a38.hu | tram 4, 6: Petőfi híd, Budai hídfő*

AKVÁRIUM (125 D1) (∅ D9)

When the sun shines through the man-made lake above, it becomes apparent how this venue got its name when the interior of the Akvárium (aquarium) is flooded by blue waves. During the day a relaxed café, bar and restaurant, in the evenings DJs mix music and there are live gigs. *Daily from noon | V | Erzsébet tér | www.akvariumklub.hu | metro 1, 2, 3: Deák Ferenc tér | tram 47, 48, 49*

AURÓRA, GÓLYA, MÜSZI

These three independent cultural centres all offer a great program of events, ranging from concerts and record fairs to exhibitions and board game parties. They are also home to civil organisations and artists. The city government has been threatening to close them for years so make sure to visit soon. *Auróra* (132 B6) (∅ G10) *(VIII | Auróra utca 11 | www.auroraonline.hu | metro 4: II János Pál pápa tér); Gólya* (136 B3) (∅ G11) *(VIII | Bókay János utca 34 | www.golyapresszo.hu | metro 3: Klinikák); Müszi* (132 A6) (∅ F9) *(VIII | Blaha Lujza tér 1 | www.muszi.org | metro 2: Blaha Lujza tér)*

ALTEREGO (131 E4) (∅ D–E8)

Budapest's most popular gay club is open to everyone. The club attracts a diverse crowd of people. A special highlight are the transvariety shows at midnight. Friday is karaoke night held in the smaller of the two rooms. *Fri 10pm–5am, Sat 10pm–6am | VI | Des-sewffy utca 33 | www.alteregoclub.hu |tram 4, 6 Oktogon*

BUDAPEST JAZZ CLUB ⭐
(131 D2) *(🛄 D6)*

Budapest's number one location for jazz warmly welcomes both newcomers and aficionados to its casual venue. Situated in the pretty district of Újlipótváros (New-Leopold Town), you can hear both Hungarian and international jazz musicians here. You can order drinks and light snacks from the tables in front of the stage while those with a larger appetite should visit its extremely tempting bistro. *XIII | Hollán Ernő utca 7 | table and ticket reservations: tel. 1 7 98 72 89 | www.bjc.hu | tram 2, 4, 6: Jászai Mari tér*

INSIDER TIP ▶ DÜRER KERT
(133 E2) *(🛄 J6)*

Kert means "garden" yet the Dürer is far more than just a great outdoor beer garden. This complex revolves around music with session rooms for fresh new talent, several live-music rooms and bars. There is always something going on from comic festivals and sweaty punk concerts to bicycle bazaars. It attracts a young crowd of guests due to the student accommodation next door. *XIV | Ajtósi Dürer sor 19–21 | www.durerkert.com | trolleybus 74, 75 Zichy Géza utca*

FOGASHÁZ (131 F5) *(🛄 E8)*

Located in an old city townhouse in Pest, this crazy party complex is not just a run-of-the-mill ruin pub, offering an entertainment centre with dart boards, table football etc. a techno club on the 1st floor, restaurant, garden and several dance floors playing a wide spectrum of music.

In 2017, the popular night club *Instant* relocated from the party mile Nagymező utca to the Fogasház. The venue often hosts concerts or DJs from abroad and attracts an international, party-loving crowd. *Daily 4pm–6pm | VII | Akácfa utca 49–51 | www.fogashaz.hu | tram 4, 6: Király utca*

DANCE & FOLKLORE

INSIDER TIP ▶ FONÓ (FONÓ BUDAI ZENEHÁZ) (0) *(🛄 C15)*

The Fonó Music House in Buda has a comprehensive, colourful culture and entertainment programme. The best time to visit is Wednesdays at 6.30pm for a session of Hungarian folk dancing – the atmosphere is unbelievable. Don't be shy; the dance instructors will show you the necessary moves. *IX | Sztregova utca 3 | www.fono.hu | tram 17, 41, 47, 48, 56, 61 Kalotaszeg utca*

NATIONAL DANCE THEATRE (NEMZETI TANC SZÍNHÁZ) (130 B5) *(🛄 B9)*

The National Dance Theatre was founded in 2001 by the Ministry of National Cultural Heritage. After years housed in the Buda Palace Theatre, the dance theatre is now homeless, forced to move out by the government who plan to move in. However you can now see the amazing dancers perform at a total of eight different venues, mainly at the Palace of Fine Arts. Current program and performances: *www.nemzetitancszinhaz.hu*

RAM COLOSSEUM (128 C6) *(🛄 D5)*

With this theatre and event complex in Pest Budapest has acquired another attractive cultural venue. Among the artists performing here is the dance group *Experidance* with their fantastic, colourful shows. *VIII | Kárpát utca 23 | www.ram colosseum.hu | trolleybus 75 from Hollan Ernő utca*

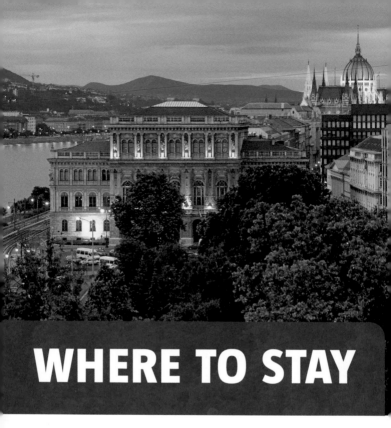

WHERE TO STAY

You can sleep well in Budapest whatever your budget. However the city's luxury hotels are a particular favourite especially among the increasing number of affluent tourists to visit the city from China and South Korea for example.

Hungary also welcomes many business tourists from Germany and France to its capital who also prefer the more exclusive four and five-star accommodation. Visitors who want a first-class experience, but not at sky-high prices, will mainly be interested in the weekend rates and the packages offered by the leading hotels. The trend for more comfort is also taking place in the mid-price range. Very basic hotels have all but disappeared, because there's hardly any demand anymore. The dividing line in the less expensive section runs between three-star hotels and guesthouses. Inexpensive accommodation is available in hostels *(www.hostelworld. com),* whose fittings are correspondingly basic, and on websites offering private accomodation (like *www.airbnb. com).*

Booking hotels directly in Budapest is significantly more expensive than doing it online. Those who do a thorough search will find deals for quite a few expensive hotels outside the main season.

There are special offers on the usual hotel reservation sites as well as on *www. budapesthotelstart.com.*

Sleep well: first-class hotels are booming, and there's a trend for a lot more comfort quite generally too

HOTELS: EXPENSIVE

ART'OTEL ★ (127 D2) (*M B8*)

The Art'otel was one of the first new design hotels to open on the Buda banks of the Danube. The best rooms in this exclusive four-star hotel are of course those with a ☼ view of the Danube and to the Parliament Building. Take the street behind the hotel past the Buda Redoute directly up to the Castle Quarter. *165 rooms | I | Bem rakpart 16–19 | tel. 1* *4 87 94 87 | www.artotels.com | metro 2: Batthyány tér | tram 19, 41*

BUDA CASTLE FASHION HOTEL

(126 B2) (*M A8*)

This small luxury oasis on Castle Hill is a real jewel. The hotel is not far from Matthias Church and blends in perfectly with the historical surroundings. All rooms are non-smoking. *25 rooms | I | Úri utca 39 | tel. 1 2 24 79 00 | www.budacastlehotelbuda-pest.com | bus 16, 16 A from Széll Kálmán tér*

Take a plunge at the relaxing Danubius Health Spa Resort Margitsziget

HILTON BUDAPEST (126 C2) (*C* B8)
This hotel is fascinating because of its location on Castle Hill (near the Fisherman's Bastion) and the incorporation of historical elements into the design. For example, you can see parts of a church nave and the tower of St Nicholas. *322 rooms | I | Hess András tér 1–3 | tel. 1 8 89 66 00 | www.budapesthilton.com | bus 16, 16A, 116*

LÁNCHÍD 19 ★ (124 A1–2) (*C* C9)
This temple of design near the Chain Bridge is an architectural tribute to glass as a building material. The interior design is inspired by the likes of Alvar Aalto and features specially created for this hotel. The foyer has a glass floor that reveals views of Roman ruins below. *47 rooms | I | Lánchíd utca 19 | tel. 1 4 19 19 00 | www.lanchid19hotel.hu | tram 19, 41: Clark Ádám tér | bus 16, 86, 105*

DANUBIUS HEALTH SPA RESORT MARGITSZIGET (128 C4) (*C* D3)
With its superb facilities, the former Margitsziget spa hotel on peaceful Margaret Island has become a stunning oasis of relaxation. Modern pools, numerous wellness therapies and beauty treatments. *267 rooms | tel. 1 8 89 47 00 | www.danubiushotels.com/margitsziget | bus 26*

MARRIOTT BUDAPEST ☆ (124 C3) (*C* D10)
This establishment keeps winning awards as a popular business hotel. And with its ten storeys it cannot be beaten when it comes to location either: all the rooms have views of the Danube. *362 rooms | V | Apáczai Csere J. utca 4 | tel. 1 4 86 50 00 | www.marriott.com | metro 1: Vörösmarty tér | tram 2: Vigadó tér*

HOTELS: MODERATE

ADINA APARTMENT HOTEL (131 E1) (*C* D6)
The Adina combines the freedom of self-catering apartments with hotel service. It has 97 apartments and studios with one or two bedrooms, a wellness centre with an indoor pool, and a breakfast room. *XIII | Hegedűs Gyula utca 52–54 | tel. 1 2 36 88 88 | www.tfehotels.com | metro 3: Lehel tér*

INSIDER TIP AMBRA (131 F5) *(ℳ E9)*
A smart little Best-Western-Plus-hotel just off the trendy Király utca. The rooms are a fine mix of comfort and contemporary design. This hotel also has apartments and hypo-allergenic rooms. *37 rooms | VII | Kis Diófa utca 13 | tel. 1 3 21 15 33 | www.hotelambra.hu | metro 1: Opera*

CONTINENTAL HOTEL BUDAPEST ★
(132 A6) (ℳ E9)
The inscription above the entrance does not give the hotel's name, instead it says *Hungária Fürdő* because it was once the magnificent Hungária Bath, built in 1827. It is situated in the Jewish Quarter and was faithfully restored a few years ago, turning it into a modern and comfortable hotel. The lobby alone is a feast for the eyes. There are two inviting courtyards and a roof garden with a large wellness area. *272 rooms | VII | Dohány utca 42–44 | tel. 1 8 15 10 00 | www.continental-hotelbudapest.com | metro 2: Blaha Lujza tér | tram 4, 6*

DANUBIUS HOTEL ASTORIA CITY CENTER *(125 E3) (ℳ E10)*
This long-established hotel was based on the New York Waldorf Astoria. It never was quite as luxurious, but a recent revamp has given its historic charm a new lustre. Pure nostalgia can be felt in the Belle Époque ambience of the *Café Astoria Restaurant*. *135 rooms | V | Kossuth Lajos utca 19–21 | tel. 1 8 89 60 00 | www.danubiushotels.com/astoria | metro 2: Astoria*

ATRIUM FASHION HOTEL
(132 B6) (ℳ F9)
The architecture and design of this hotel create a bright atmosphere that is flooded with light. A lot of white and lovely shades of turquoise, blue and yellow give it an elegant, cheerful feel.

57 rooms | VIII | Csokonai utca 14 | tel. 1 2 99 0/ 77 | www.atriumhotelbudapest.com | metro 2: Blaha Lujza tér

CASATI BUDAPEST HOTEL
(131 E5) (ℳ E8)
One of the oldest houses in Terézváros was transformed into a gem by the owners, who are architects. They integrated parts of the old stonework into the building and restored the beautiful old courtyard as well. Not far away from Andrássy út. *25 rooms | VI | Paulay Ede utca 31 | tel. 1 3 43 11 98 | www.casatibudapesthotel.com | metro 1: Opera*

INSIDER TIP CENTRAL BASILICA
(131 D5) (ℳ D9)
Both the location and the room prices are excellent. Situated right by St Ste-

MARCO POLO HIGHLIGHTS

★ **Art'otel**
Stylish designer hotel on the Buda banks of the Danube → p. 83

★ **Lánchíd 19**
Designer highlight with an unusual glass façade → p. 84

★ **Continental Hotel Budapest**
A luxury oasis in the former Hungária Bath dating from 1827 → p. 85

★ **Four Seasons Gresham Palace**
Art Nouveau building with a stunningly beautiful interior → p. 86

★ **Full Moon Design Hostel Budapest**
Ultra-modern hostel with its own courtyard club → p. 89

phen's Basilica (on the car-free fore-court of the magnificent church), this hotel has the best three-star levels of comfort. *46 rooms | V | Hercegprimás utca 8 | tel. 1 328 50 10 | www.hotel centralbasilica.hu | metro 1: Bajcsy-Zsi-linszky út*

DANUBIUS HOTEL ERZSÉBET CITY CENTER (125 E4) (*Ø D10*)

This hotel, opened in 1873, has a perfect city-centre location and has been com-pletely modernised, from the rooms' interiors to the technology. Guests will find an upscale three-star establishment. *123 rooms | V | Károlyi utca 11–15 | tel. 1 889 37 00 | www.danubiushotels.com/ erzsebet | metro 3: Ferenciek tere*

K + K HOTEL OPERA (131 E5) (*Ø D8*)

It's the big names who've inspired the design here – Le Corbusier, Eileen Gray, Charles Eames, Philippe Starck. Service and atmosphere deserve top marks. The bistro bar is a popular meeting place. *206 rooms | VI | Révay utca 24 | tel. 1 269 02 22 | www.kkhotels.com | metro 1: Opera*

MAMAISON RESIDENCE IZABELLA (131 F4) (*Ø E7*)

Many of the generously sized (45–97 sq m) feel-good apartments, which are decked out with wooden floors, look out onto the pretty courtyard and have a balcony. The house has a sauna and a gym. The inviting 19th-century build-

MORE THAN A GOOD NIGHT'S SLEEP

The art of sleeping …

… is to be understood literally at the boutique hotel INSIDER TIP *Brody House* **(125 F3)** (*Ø E10*) *(11 rooms | VIII | Bródy Sándor utca 10 | tel. 1 266 12 11 | brody-house.com | metro 3: Kálvin tér | Mode-rate)*: the rooms are all individually fur-nished, some of which in an extremely extravagant design. Breakfast is served in the salon which also contains a casu-al bar. Dating from 1896, the building has always been home to artists. The *Artist Residencies* are today held in the associat-ed *Brody Studios* (VI | Vörösmarty utca 38) which also has its own private club – ask nicely and they might let you in!

Establishment with vintage charm

Painter and designer Ádám Szarvas and his team have created the absolute feel-good hostel for individualistic dream-ers in the INSIDER TIP *Lavender Circus*

Hostel **(125 F4)** (*Ø E10*) *(15 twin rooms | V | Múzeum körút 37 | tel. 70 417 77 63 | www.lavendercircus.com | metro 3, 4: Kálvin tér | tram 47, 48, 49 | Budget)*.It feels like a cosy flat shared by artists with a lot of love to detail. This centrally locat-ed yet quiet hostel is very family friendly – there is space in each room for a cot.

Art Nouveau to dream of

No exaggeration, the ⭐ *Four Seasons Gresham Palace* **(124 B1)** (*Ø C9*) *(169 rooms | V | Széchenyi István tér 5–6 | tel. 1 268 60 00 | www.fourseasons.com/bu-dapest | metro 1: Vörösmarty tér | tram 2 | Expensive)* is Budapest's most stunning hotel. No surprise then that rock and Hol-lywood stars have spent the night here (including the Red Hot Chili Peppers, An-thony Hopkins). You can take a peek in-side by treating yourself to the *Herend Af-ternoon Tea (daily 3pm–6pm)*.

Guests are treated to art galore at the Brody House

ing is not far from Andrássy út boulevard. *38 suites | VI | Izabella utca 61 | tel. 1 475 59 00 | www.mamaisonizabella. com | metro 1: Vörösmarty utca*

MERCURE KORONA (125 E4) *(ρ E10)*
Favourably located (for transport) on the Small Boulevard (Kiskörút), this hotel, with comparatively small rooms, benefits from the lively atmosphere of its surroundings. *424 rooms | V | Kecskeméti utca 14 | tel. 1 486 88 00 | www. mercure-korona.hu | metro 3, 4: Kálvin tér | tram 47, 49*

INSIDER TIP SOHO BOUTIQUE HOTEL (132 A5) *(ρ F9)*
The blue, yellow and orange façade lighting is a clear signal in the evenings that the Soho has brought a touch of avant-garde into Dohány utca. Retro colours

and retro design also set the tone in the lobby bar. The rooms are painted in more muted tones and are very comfortable and well equipped (e.g. with large-format TV screens). *74 rooms | VII | Dohány utca 64 | tel. 1 872 82 92 | www. sohoboutiquehotel.com | metro 2: Baha Lujza tér | tram 4, 6*

HOTELS: BUDGET & GUESTHOUSES

CORVIN PLAZA APARTMENTS AND SUITES (136 B2) *(ρ F11)*
If you like your own space, and this includes when you're on holiday, the Corvin Plaza is the right place for you. With 45 modern and tastefully decorated apartments and suites, you can choose which room type best suits you. Many of the apartments have a balcony or terrace. Pets

Vibrant district in the city: the trendy mile Ráday utca, where the Hotel Ibis Centrum is located

and children are welcome (you can even ask to borrow a cot and pushchair). Parking spaces and online discounts available! *VIII | Kisfaludy utca 3 | tel. 20 3 65 74 88 | www.corvinbp.com | metro 3: Corvin-negyed | tram 4, 6 | Budget*

HOTEL SHIP FORTUNA
(131 D1–2) *(മ D5–6)*
Enjoying the Danube close up while having breakfast on the terrace: this is possible on the *Fortuna*. The boat is located on the Pest side of the city opposite Margaret Island. The rooms (on the upper deck) have good three-star comfort levels. The best rooms are the four ☀☀ superior rooms, which also have stunning views. There is an inexpensive hostel with 14 rooms downstairs and an affiliated restaurant. *56 rooms | XIII | Szent István Park | Alsó rakpart | tel. 1 2 88 81 00 | www.fortunahajo.hu | tram 2, 4, 6 | trolleybus 75, 76*

IBIS CENTRUM (125 F5) *(മ E11)*
The service and the entire ambience of this hotel in the Ráday utca shopping and party area is very friendly. It's also excellent value for money. *126 rooms | IX | Ráday utca 6 | tel. 1 4 56 41 00 | www.ibis-centrum.hu | metro 3, 4: Kálvin tér*

CITY HOTEL MÁTYÁS (125 D4) *(മ D10)*
Breakfast is served in the famous *Matthias Cellar* with its opulent decor – the hotel is situated above the long established restaurant. Only 50 m/164 ft away is the shopping mile Váci utca. *85 rooms | V | Március 15. tér 8 | tel. 1 3 18 05 95 | www.cityhotel.hu | metro 3: Ferenciek tere | tram 2*

HOTEL MOLNÁR (0) *(മ 0)*
Situated on the slopes of the Széchenyi mountain this hotel offers a getaway from the city's hustle and bustle and you can take a deep breath even in summer.

The appealing offers comprise a restaurant and a sauna. 15 rooms with balconies. With the bus you can reach the tram intersection Újbuda-központ in just 20 minutes. *23 rooms | XII | Fodor utca 143 | tel. 1 3 95 18 72 | www.hotelmolnarbudapest. hu | bus 53 from Újbuda-központ*

INSIDER TIP STAR CITY HOTEL
(132 C4) (ɯ G8)

The neighbourhood is still fairly dull, but the hotel itself has been completely renovated inside and out. It has a young, fresh atmosphere and also has family rooms (rooms with connecting doors). The central location and the fair prices are further benefits. *48 rooms | VII | István utca 14 | tel. 1 479 04 20 | www.star hotel.hu | metro 2, 4: Keleti Pályaudvar*

STAR INN HOTEL *(131 E4) (ɯ D–E8)*

In a quiet lane between Andrássy út and the West Railway Station, the Budapest branch of this hotel chain offers solid no-frills accomodation. Friendly atmosphere; only a few minutes to the opera or the nightlife on Liszt Ferenc tér. Standard and business rooms; also rooms with twin beds. *119 rooms | VI | Dessewffy utca 36 | tel. 1 4 72 20 20 | www.starinnhotels. com | metro 1: Oktogon | metro 3: Arany János utca*

HOSTELS

FULL MOON DESIGN HOSTEL BUDAPEST ★ *(131 D3) (ɯ D7)*

Hostel and design combined in one? Indeed at the Full Moon Design Hostel! The Full Moon is stylishly furnished from the ground to the third floor. The building has been fully renovated and sightseeing attractions and the pretty district of Újlipótváros are close by. If you like to party, the *Morrison's 2* club is located in the hostel's courtyard and admission is free to guests. *54 rooms | V | Szent István körút 11 | tel. 30 3 26 68 88 | www. fullmoonhostel.com | metro 3: Nyugati pályaudvar | tram 2, 4, 6: Jászai Mari tér | Budget*

WOMBAT'S CITY HOSTEL
(125 E1) (ɯ D9)

Hostel situated in a beautifully renovated old building in the heart of the former Jewish quarter. High standard and various extras such as free towels, a baggage storage room and a guest kitchen. More than 450 beds, in dormitories (up to 8 beds, from approx. 3,000 Ft.) as well as in double rooms (from approx. 12,000 Ft.). Breakfast buffet costs 1,100 Ft. extra. *VI | Király utca 20 | tel. 1 8 83 50 05 | www.wombats-hostels.com | metro 1, 2, 3: Deák Ferenc tér*

LOW BUDGET

During the Sziget Festival, the rooms in the *Bánki* **(131 E4) *(ɯ D7–8)* *(31 rooms | VI | Podmaniczky utca 8 | tel. 20 7 76 22 64 | metro 3: Nyugati pályaudvar)* are high in demand (per person in a double room 4,600 Ft., during the festival 5,300 Ft.). The four storeys (in a student residence) are only open in July and August.

The *Hotel Medosz* **(131 F4) *(ɯ E8)* *(70 rooms | VI | Jókai tér | tel. 1 3 74 30 00 | www.medoszhotel.hu | tram 4, 6 | metro 1: Oktogon)* offers pleasantly renovated rooms in a good location. Students and pensioners get a 10% discount. Double rooms 1,500–2,500 Ft. (incl. breakfast buffet).

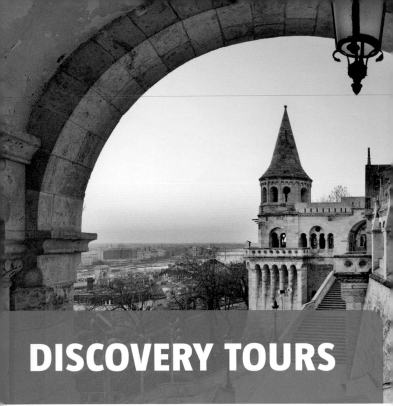

DISCOVERY TOURS

① BUDAPEST AT A GLANCE

START: ① Deák Ferenc tér END: ① Deák Ferenc tér	1 day Walking and travelling time (without stops) 3 hours
Distance: 🚇 18 km/11 miles	

COSTS: Public transport ticket 1,650 Ft. (24-hour ticket, included if you have a Budapest Card)
WHAT TO PACK: swimwear

IMPORTANT TIPS:
Matthias Church: often closed on Saturday afternoons for weddings, no visitors allowed on Sunday mornings during church service

Budapest is a fascinating city with many different faces. This one-day tour offers a diverse choice of attractions for you to see and a good insight into Hungary's

Would you like to explore the places that are unique to this city? Then the Discovery Tours are just the thing for you – they include terrific tips for stops worth making, breathtaking places to visit, selected restaurants and fun activities. It's even easier with the Touring App: download the tour with map and route to your smartphone using the QR Code on pages 2/3 or from the website address in the footer below – and you'll never get lost again even when you're offline. → p. 2/3

TOURING APP

capital. You'll discover and experience all the delights that define Budapest, from its historic Castle Quarter to the trendy bars in the former Jewish district.

09:00am Start your day in Budapest with a trip to the Castle Quarter in Buda. The best place to start your tour is the central traffic junction ❶ **Deák Ferenc tér** at the centre of the Pest side of the city. **From there, take bus 16 over the ❷ Chain Bridge → p. 37 to the Buda side of the city.** From the funicular station *(Sikló)*, the bus makes its ascent up ❸ **Castle Hill**, where you get off at the Dísz tér bus stop.

METRO 1, 2, 3	
❶ Deák Ferenc tér	
❷ Chain Bridge	🏛

BUS 16 DÍSZ TÉR	
❸ Castle Hill	
🏰🏠🏛🌳☕	

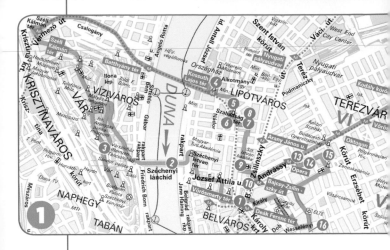

On your left is the impressive **Buda Palace → p. 29 and if you follow Tárnok utca on your right to Szentháromság tér,** two highlights are awaiting you there.

10:00am The majestic **Matthias church → p. 33** stands on Szentháromság tér with the **Fisherman's Bastion → p. 30** in front providing wonderful views over the city. Take a short coffee break **on Szentháromság utca** at the famous Biedermeier café **Ruszwurm Cukrászda** *(daily | Szentháromság utca 7 | www.ruszwurm.hu)* before enjoying a relaxing stroll **along Hess András tér and Fortuna utca to Bécsi kapu tér.**

11:30am Take the bus (16, 16A, 116) from Bécsi kapu tér to Széll Kálmán tér and from there the metro line 2 to Kossuth Lajos tér by the **④ Parliament Building → p. 38.** A walk through the streets of **Leopold Town** *(Lipótváros)* will sum up the meaning of the term "eclecticism" beautifully: the different architectural styles come together to produce a visual treat. **Head along Báthory utca and go right on Honvéd utca** where house number 3 is the **⑤ House of Hungarian Art Nouveau (Magyar szecesszió háza)** *(closed Sun | www.magyarszecessziohaza.hu)* with its splendid Art Nouveau façade and an authentic Art Nouveau **café** for an energizing coffee break. A few feet away is the park-like **⑥ Szabadság tér → p. 39** with splendid buildings dating back to the period of rapid industrial expansion in

BUS 16, 16A, 116 AND
METRO 2 KOSSUTH LAJOS TÉR

④ Parliament Building
🏛

⑤ House of Hungarian Art Nouveau
🏛 ☕

⑥ Szabadság tér
🎧 🏛

DISCOVERY TOURS

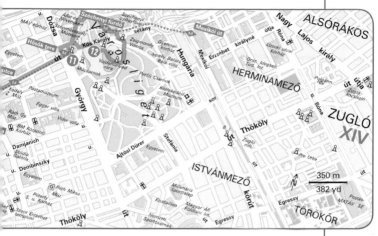

Europe. **Go past the US embassy and take a left along Hold utca** where you will be confronted with a masterpiece designed by the architect Ödön Lechner: the former **❼ Post Office Savings Bank** *(Magyar Király Takarék Pénztár)*, which is today part of the National Bank. Directly opposite is the nice **❽ indoor market hall** where you can stock up on your supplies with food from Hungarian small businesses.

`01:00pm` **Head south following Hercegprímás utca to ❾ St Stephen's Basilica → p. 39.** Stop for a moment on **Szent István tér**: the view of this neoclassical basilica with its enormous dome is almost as beautiful as the church's interior. Stop for lunch at one of the many cafés in this quarter.

`02:00pm` **❿ Andrássy út → p. 41 starts behind the basilica on the left** and the underground station Bajcsy-Zsilinszky út is situated there. The historic **underground line 1** *(Földalatti)* is an ideal way to explore this exclusive avenue. On **⓫ Heroes' Square → p. 43** (Hősök tere stop) where you will also find the **Millennium Memorial,** you will be right in the midst of Hungarian history. This place also has some great art to offer in the **Museum of Fine Arts → p. 44** with its own **café**.

`03:30pm` **From Heroes' Square, it's just a few feet to the ⓬ municipal forest → p. 45** with its many attrac-

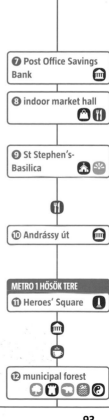

❼ Post Office Savings Bank

❽ indoor market hall

❾ St Stephen's-Basilica

❿ Andrássy út

METRO 1 HŐSÖK TERE
⓫ Heroes' Square

⓬ municipal forest

93

tions such as the romantic **Vajdahunyad Castle** → p. 46 or the **Budapest Zoo** → p. 42. Feeling tired? Then relax your mind and body in the palatial **Széchenyi Baths** → p. 45 (follow the signposts).

05:30pm **Take the metro line 1 back to the Opera at Andrássy út.** All around the magnificent ⑬ **Opera House** → p. 45 reside shops and restaurants, characterised by exquisite architecture. Time for a refreshment? Uniquely designed, crazy sweet treats, ice cream and coffee as well as quirky bric-a-brac is available **nearby at** ⑭ **INSIDER TIP Sugar!** *(daily | Paulay Ede utca 48 | www.sugarshop.hu)*. It is worthwhile to have a look inside if you like colours!

07:00pm A few feet away is ⑮ **Liszt Ferenc tér** → p. 44 with a wide selection of cafés for eating and drinking including **Menza** → p. 65.

09:00pm Liszt Ferenc tér is also inviting for an evening drink and is the ideal starting point for a stroll around the former Jewish Quarter. **Go along Király utca and then take a left into Kazinczy utca** with its many cafés such as the alternative bar ⑯ **Szimpla kert** → p. 77. Other alternatives are the lively cafés in the Gozsdu Court → p. 47 located on Kiraly utca before returning to ❶ **Deák Ferenc tér**.

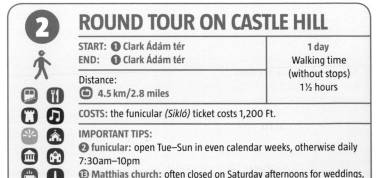

2 ROUND TOUR ON CASTLE HILL

START: ❶ Clark Ádám tér END: ❶ Clark Ádám tér	1 day Walking time (without stops) 1½ hours
Distance: 🚠 4.5 km/2.8 miles	

COSTS: the funicular *(Sikló)* ticket costs 1,200 Ft.

IMPORTANT TIPS:
❷ **funicular:** open Tue–Sun in even calendar weeks, otherwise daily 7:30am–10pm
⑬ **Matthias church:** often closed on Saturday afternoons for weddings, no visitors allowed on Sunday mornings during church service

Castle Hill rises 60 m (almost 200 ft) above the banks of the Danube. Despite all the disasters that have struck this historic core of the city such as earthquakes, fires, sieges and wars, the hill, which is 1.5 km (1 mile) long and up to 500 m (1,640 ft) wide, is a gem of cultural history. Two-thirds of the area is taken up by the Castle Quarter, the other third by the enormous Buda Palace.

`09:00am` From **❶ Clark Ádám tér** (by the Chain Bridge on the Buda side of the river), the nicest (if not the cheapest) way to get up Castle Hill is to take the **❷ funicular** *(Sikló)*. During the two-minute trip it travels 101 m/331 ft on a 48 percent gradient, up **to Szent György tér.** Alternatively – and free –, you can walk up in ten minutes on the `INSIDER TIP` **path left of the** *Sikló* **starting point**, past a giant mosaic of Hungary's coat of arms.

At the funicular's top station, turn left to ❸ Buda Castle → p. 29 with its excellent museums. The **Hungarian National Gallery** → p. 34 offers an impressive exhibition of Hungarian art from the medieval period onwards. The **Matthias Fountain**, situated next to the building at the entrance to the History Museum's courtyard, depicts the legend of the peasant girl on the left of the fountain, Ilona (according to some sources Ilonka), who encountered the king when he was out hunting incognito, and fell in love with him. After she discovered that she had fallen in love with a man who was beyond her reach, she is said to have died of a broken heart.

The funicular takes you from Clark Ádám tér up Castle Hill

Back at the funicular's top station, you will notice the neoclassical **❹ Sándor Palace** *(Sándor palota)* built in 1806 and the official residence of the President of the Republic of Hungary. The neighbouring palace was a former Carmelite monastery and was transformed into Buda's first

❶ Clark Ádám tér

❷ funicular

FUNICULAR SZENT GYÖRGY TÉR

❸ Buda Castle

❹ Sándor Palace

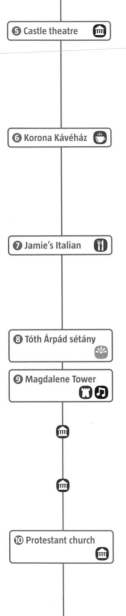

⑤ Castle theatre 🏛

⑥ Korona Kávéház ☕

⑦ Jamie's Italian 🍴

⑧ Tóth Árpád sétány 🌼

⑨ Magdalene Tower 🎪🎵

🏛

🏛

⑩ Protestant church 🏛

permanent theatre at the behest of Emperor Joseph II in 1790. The **⑤ Castle theatre** *(Várszínház)* housed the National Dance Theatre for decades and now the Prime Minister plans to open his new residence here.

Now head along Szent György utca to Dísz tér (Parade Square) which once marked the boundary between the Castle Quarter and the area where the commoners lived. During the Middle Ages, markets as well as executions were held on the square. **⑥ Korona Kávéház** *(daily | Dísz tér 16)* and **Vár Bisztró** *(daily | Dísz tér 8)* invite you to take a coffee or snack break here.

01:00pm **Several streets lead off from Dísz tér including Úri utca (Lord's Street).** On **Szentháromság utca** (Holy Trinity Street) you will notice the Matthias Church on the right which you will go past on your way back. In this lane you'll also find **⑦ Jamie's Italian** *(daily | Szentháromság utca 9–11 | tel. 1 8 00 92 12 | www.jamieoliver.com/italian/hungary),* Jamie Oliver's Italian franchise restaurant, where you can treat yourself to a lunch of antipasti and pizza on the terrace.

Continue the walk left along Szentháromság utca to ⑧ Tóth Árpád sétány, a promenade on the defensive walls of Castle Hill with good views of the hills on the Buda side of the city. **Follow the promenade to the pretty Kapisztrán tér** with the late-Gothic **⑨ Magdalene Tower** *(Magdolna torony)*, which plays a carillon every quarter of an hour. Only the tower of the church (13th century) managed to avoid destruction in World War II. The neoclassical **Museum of Military History** *(Hadtörténeti Múzeum)* was once a barracks.

Behind the church tower, Országház utca heads right to the old Regional parliament building. The Hungarian assembly was held here between 1785 and 1806. Take a stroll **along the small Kard utca to Fortuna utca. Go left to get to Bécsi kapu tér** (Vienna Gate Square). On the corner is the neoclassical **⑩ Protestant church**.

The north-eastern part of Castle Quarter was the Jewish ghetto during the Middle Ages. **Its centre Táncsics Mihály utca (junction of Bécsi kapu tér),** was commonly known as the "Jewish Lane". Remnants of Jewish life in the Middle Ages are exhibited in the

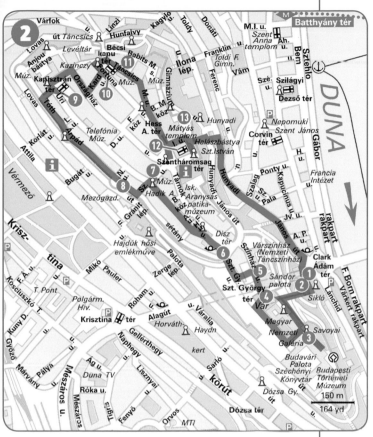

⑪ **Medieval Jewish House of Prayer** (no. 26) which is open during the summer months. Its most beautiful Baroque building is **Erdődy Palace** (no. 7). The street ends at the square in front of the Hotel Hilton, the Hess Andras tér. It owes its name to the 15th century German painter, Andreas Hess, who is said to have produced the first book to be printed in Hungary.

From here it is just a few steps to the impressive ⑫ **Matthias church** → p. 33 on Szentháromság tér (Trinity Square). The 14 m/46 ft high **Holy Trinity Column** on the square was erected in 1715 to commemorate the ravages of the plague in 1706.

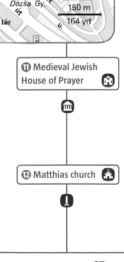

⑪ Medieval Jewish House of Prayer

⑫ Matthias church

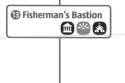

⑱ Fisherman's Bastion

Behind the church stretches the extremely photogenic **⑱ Fisherman's Bastion** → p. 30. It offers a splendid view over the Danube to the Parliament Building. The large **equestrian statue** of King Stephen I is another work by sculptor Alajos Stróbl (1856–1926), who also designed the Matthias Fountain. This part of Castle Hill – Matthias Church, Fisherman's Bastion and the equestrian statue – was designed and implemented towards the end of the 19th century by Frigyes Schulek as an entire complex.

❶ Clark Ádám tér

`05:00pm` The way back leads from the Fisherman's Bastion, down the **Royal stairs** (Király lépcső) **) to the Hunyadi János út,** which ends at your starting point at **❶ Clark Ádám tér.**

③ ELISABETH TOWN: IN THE OLD JEWISH QUARTER

START: ❶ Deák Ferenc tér END: ❶ Deák Ferenc tér	½ day Walking time (without stops) 1½ hours
Distance: 🚶 4 km/2.5 miles	
IMPORTANT TIPS: Synagogues are closed on the Sabbath (Saturday) and close earlier on Friday afternoons	

Located between the Small and Large Central City Rings, Elisabeth Town has become a very fashionable district in Budapest. While some places embrace both decay and new development, things are getting more colourful and lively every year. There is plenty of luxury around, as in the new fashionable hotels, fine shops, restaurants and bars, but there is also a young, alternative scene.

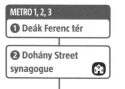

METRO 1, 2, 3

❶ Deák Ferenc tér

❷ Dohány Street synagogue

The walk around the Jewish quarter starts at the central traffic junction **❶ Deák Ferenc tér. From there, cross the Small Central Ring (here: Károly körút)** to the religious centre of the Jewish community, the splendid **❷ Dohány Street Synagogue** → p. 49, which was ceremonially inaugurated in 1859.

Before World War II, Budapest was home to around 200,000 Jews. At the end of 1944, Elisabeth Town, sealed off by the Nazis and the Hungarian Arrow Cross

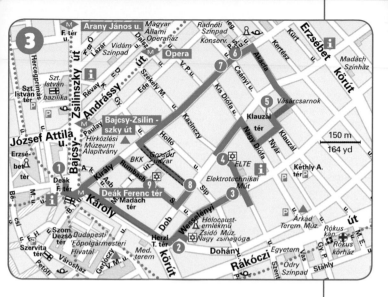

Party from the surrounding area by a wall, became a ghetto, and for the thousands of Jews confined within it, this became a grave. The Holocaust Memorial Centre → p. 50 and the glimmering, silver **Holocaust memorial** by artist Imre Varga in the courtyard of the synagogue are poignant reminders of this crime.

Today there are around 80,000 Jews in Budapest, most of them living spread out over the entire city. But Elisabeth Town is a quarter in which Jewish life has left many marks and in which Jewish religion and tradition have become a vital force again. Get to know more about all this in the **Jewish Museum** housed in one of the synagogue's wings.

From the front of the synagogue (Theodor-Herzl Square), follow Wesselényi utca. If you keep going down this street, you will pass, among other places, Jewish shops and cafés. It is worth taking a break at **3** INSIDERTIP **Noé Cukrászda** (daily | Wesselényi utca 13) where you can find delicious Jewish pastries such as the traditional *flódni* (layers of walnuts, apple, poppy seed and plum jam).

3 Noé Cukrászda

Finally you'll reach the Kazinczy utca that was traffic calmed in the last years after having been declared a

4 Orthodox Synagogue

"cultural zone". To the right is the ruin pub Szimpla kert → p. 77, but you'll go to the left where you will reach the excellently renovated **4 Orthodox Synagogue** → **p. 48** that lies in a building complex reaching right up to the Dob utca. This area is full of restaurants, cafés and pubs.

The walk now takes you right along the Dob utca to Klauzál tér where you can have a snack (e.g. *lángos)* in the small **5 indoor market hall** where you can also buy some fruit, tasty cheese and bread. **At the other end of the street, turn left along Akácfa utca to the 6 Terezvaros Parish Church** on Király utca. The tower was built by architect Miklós Ybl (who also designed the Opera House) in 1871.

5 indoor market hall

6 Terezvaros Parish Church

Splendid construction: inside the synagogue on Dohány utca

7 Király utca

If you now take a left along 7 Király utca you will find yourself in the middle of a fascinating refurbishment process. A citizens' initiative managed to save many of the houses from demolition yet many private owners and the city district still lack the necessary financial aid for the refurbishment. The consequence being that rows of historical buildings were replaced with faceless new buildings. In the lower part of the street, **towards Deák Ferenc tér,** the tone is set by design shops such as **Goa** *(no. 21)* or the flower and decor shop **Arioso** *(no. 9 | www. arioso.hu).*

After many years of decay, the wonderful complex in number 13, the **Gozsdu Court** → p. 47, has been restored to its former glory. After luxury apartment lets failed to bring expected profits, numerous cafés and bars have relocated to this complex. This is a popular destination in the evening.

On the opposite side of the Gozsdu Court, take a right along Dob utca. On the other side of the street is ❽ **Spinoza** → p. 65, a popular address for a coffee or snacks. This café-restaurant is also known for its Klezmer evenings every Friday. **Take a right at the next crossroads along Rumbach Sebestyén utca.** The ❾ **Rumbach Synagogue** → p. 49 was designed by Viennese architect Otto Wagner in 1872, in Romanesque-Moorish style; it is still in need of a few renovations.

At the end of the street, turn left into Király utca again, which ends at the Small Central Ring. On the right ahead, you will reach your starting point on ❶ **Deák Ferenc tér**.

❽ Spinoza

❾ Rumbach Synagogue

❶ Deák Ferenc tér

4 · BOAT TOUR ON THE DANUBE

START: ❶ Vörösmarty tér **END:** ❶ Vörösmarty tér	½ day Travelling and walking time (without stops) 2 ¼ hours
Distance: 🚶 9.5 km/5.9 miles	

COSTS:
Public transport costs 1,650 Ft. (24-hour ticket, included if you have a Budapest Card, liners and cruise ships also included Mon–Fri)
Liner costs 750 Ft. (single trip, Sat/Sun or without BKK season ticket)
WHAT TO PACK: swimwear

IMPORTANT TIPS:
Liners D11 and D12 leave daily approx. every 30–60 minutes. Another line (D13) operates at weekends in Summer. Remember to check the timetable before your journey: *www.bkk.hu*

Budapest is dominated by the Danube. The river flows through the city centre and many of the tourist attractions are located on the banks of this large European river. No wonder that its fantastic panoramic is now included in the UNESCO list of World Heritage Sites. On this combined tour by tram, boat and on foot, you can enjoy the unique flair of this capital from the river.

METRO 1

❶ Vörösmarty tér

❷ Vigadó tér

❸ Hungarian Academy of Sciences

Starting point is the central i**❶ Vörösmarty tér** → p. 41 on the Pest side of the Danube. From here **head left along Vigadó utca to the Danube promenade at ❷ Vigadó tér.** Behind you is the prestigious **Pest Redoubt** → p. 39, and in front of you on the opposite banks of the Danube is the monumental **Buda Castle** → p. 29.

At Vigadó tér, take tram line 2 northwards towards Jászai Mari tér. The journey alone is worth it for the splendid panoramic views over to the Buda banks of the Danube. The tram first takes you along Széchenyi István tér under the ramp up the Chain Bridge → p. 37 and then passes the **❸ Hungarian Academy of Sciences** → p. 40.

Sightseeing from the river: The liners also dock at the Parliament Building

The journey continues to Kossuth Lajos tér which was completely redesigned and from where you can appreciate the front side of the **❹ Parliament Building → p. 38** in its full splendour. **Get off the tram at the end of the line on Jászai Mari tér and cross the Large Central Ring,** the busy access road to the Margaret Bridge.

When you reach the other side, go left down to the Danube where you will see the **Jászai Mari tér jetty** on your right. On the opposite banks you will spot Margaret Island → p. 37. The white liners have been crossing the Danube since 2012. No running commentary is provided on the boats, however they do stop at several stations along the route.

❹ Parliament Building

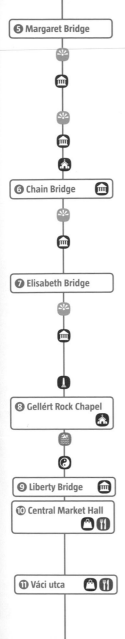

⑤ Margaret Bridge

⑥ Chain Bridge

⑦ Elisabeth Bridge

⑧ Gellért Rock Chapel

⑨ Liberty Bridge

⑩ Central Market Hall

⑪ Váci utca

The boat trip heading south first takes you under the **⑤ Margaret Bridge** and across to the **Kossuth Lajos tér jetty** directly at the southern end of the Parliament Building. On the way you will be treated to fantastic views on your left of the impressive **Parliament Building → p. 38.** The next stop, the **Batthyány tér jetty,** is located on the Buda side of the Danube.

The journey continues downstream. On your right is the Castle Quarter with the **Fisherman's Bastion → p. 30** behind which stands the royal **Matthias church → p. 33,** before sailing underneath the elegant **⑥ Chain Bridge → p. 37.** This was Budapest's first permanent bridge to cross the Danube and is still one of the city's landmarks today. The vast **Buda Castle → p. 29** will now grab your full attention while the boat approaches the **Várkert bazár jetty** located beneath the castle grounds. The journey then continues on the Pest banks of the Danube to the **Petőfi tér jetty.**

Set sail again past the white **⑦ Elisabeth Bridge**. Above the Turkish **Rudas thermal baths → p. 34** towers the steep **Gellért Hill → p. 32.** At the top of the hill you will clearly recognise the **Citadel → p. 32** and the **Liberty Statue → p. 32.**

The boat will dock directly after the green Liberty Bridge on the right below the Gellért Thermal Baths and Hotel at the **Szent Gellért tér jetty** on the Buda side of the Danube. Climb out here to visit the prettily located **⑧ Gellért Rock Chapel → p. 33.** First enjoy a relaxing break in the hot thermal water at the **Gellért thermal baths → p. 32.**

Then take a stroll over the ⑨ Liberty Bridge → p. 50 to cross the Danube back to the Pest side. The **⑩ Central Market Hall → p. 71** is situated on Fővám tér with its colourful selection of peppers, salami etc. and is a real experience for the senses. If you fancy a quick bite, try the delicious *lángos,* fried pita bread with a selection of fillings, sold on the first floor.

Heading north, follow the ⑪ Váci utca → p. 40 shopping mile. To the north, at the crossroads with Szabadsajto ut, you will find the small shop INSIDERTIP **Molnár's Kürtőskalács** *(daily | Váci utca 31 | www.kurtoskalacs. com),* where you can buy the traditional spit cake, or tree cake *(kürtőskalács)*, a very popular sweet pastry in Hungary which is hollow inside.

Now take a quick detour and **head left along Piarista köz street to the ⑫ Inner City Parish Church → p. 37 and around the Március 15. Tér designed like a city park. Back on Váci utca, take a left** to return to the starting point of this tour, the ❶ **Vörösmarty tér → p. 41**.

⑫ Inner City Parish Church

❶ Vörösmarty tér

At the Gellért thermal baths, you could almost forget to swim for all the Art Nouveau around

TRAVEL WITH KIDS

BUDAPEST ZOO (BUDAPESTI ÁLLATKERT) (132 B1–2) (𝄞 F–G 6)

A kids' paradise with petting zoo, many fun activities and 3,000 animals (700 species). Special programme every June on "Museum Night". *May–Aug Mon–Thu 9am–6pm, Fri–Sun 9am–7pm, otherwise daily 9am–4pm (March, Oct until 5pm; April, Sept until 5:30pm) | admission 2,800 Ft., children 1,900 Ft., family ticket (2 adults, 2 children) 7,900 Ft. | XIV | Állatkerti körút 6–12 | www.zoobudapest.com | metro 1: Széchenyi fürdő*

CHILDRENS' RAILWAY (GYERMEKVASÚT) (138 C4–5) (𝄞 O)

The narrow-gauge railway is operated by children (under supervision). The track through the woods is 11 km (7 miles) long. To get here take tram 59 or 61 from Széll Kálmán tér to the cog railway station *(Városmajor)*, which leads up Széchenyi-hegy hill. From here you can walk to the railway. Its stations are good starting points for hikes into the Buda Hills. The second terminal station Hűvösvölgy can be reached directly by taking tram 61 departing from Széll Kálmán tér. *May–Aug daily 9am–7pm, Sept–April Tue–Sun 9am–5pm | single ticket 700 Ft., children 350 Ft. | www.gyermekvasut.hu*

HUNGARIAN NATURAL HISTORY MUSEUM (MAGYAR TERMÉSZETTU-DOMÁNYI MÚZEUM) (136 C3) (𝄞 H12)

The dinosaur park can already be seen from outside. The museum is tailored to children: there are many interactive games, simulated landscapes with animals, an underwater hall and lots more. The choice is rather too big. *Wed–Mon 10am–6pm | Ticket for all exhibitions 2,000 Ft., children 1,000 Ft. | VIII | Ludovika tér 2–6 | www.nhmus.hu | metro 3: Klinikák*

HUNGARIAN RAILWAY MUSEUM (MAGYAR VASÚTTÖRTÉNETI PARK) (139 D4) (𝄞 J2)

Adventure park with engine simulator, draisine ride and model railways. Rarities include a steam engine built in 1870 and a dining car from the Orient Express dating back to 1912. The excursion trains running from the West Railway Station (Nyugati pályaudvar) to Esztergom stop at the museum's train station *Vasútmúzeum* three times a day. *April–Oct Tue–Sun 10am–6pm, mid–late March, Nov 10am–3pm | admission 1,700 Ft., children 800 Ft., family ticket (2 adults, 2 children) 4,000 Ft. | XIV | Tatai út 95 | www.vasuttorteneti park.hu | bus 30 from Hősök tere*

Splashing around, being amazed, feeding animals: from flumes to petting zoos, there's lots to experience for young visitors to Budapest

INSIDER TIP KÁROLYI KERT
(125 E3–4) (*ø E10*)

Quiet, secluded oasis in the middle of Pest city centre. This small park is surrounded by wrought-iron fencing and dogs are not allowed so it is safe for youngsters to run around. Kids have a choice of two playgrounds while mums and dads can enjoy a refreshing lemonade or a *cold brew* at one of the surrounding cafes. Child and parent-friendly! *V | Ferenczy István utca | metro 2: Astoria | tram 47, 49*

ON TOUR WITH A BRINGÓMOBIL
(128 B4) (*ø D3*)

You can hire these funny open vehicles on Margaret Island, where you can easily spend an entire day. *Bringós* can be hired for small children or families; electric or pedal-powered versions are available. *Bringóhintó Margitsziget | pedal mobile from 3,880 Ft., childrens' mobile from 2,480 Ft., electromobile from 5,580 Ft. per hour | Alfréd sétány 1 | www.bringo hinto.hu | bus 26, 226*

PALATINUS BATHS (PALATINUS FÜRDŐ)
(128 B4–5) (*ø C4*)

This outdoor pool in a large park, with its eleven pools (also wave pool), four 400 ft slides and kamikaze flume offers a lot of entertainment. During high summer it tends to be very full. *Mid-June–mid Sept daily 9am–7pm (until Aug 20 until 8pm) | admission Mon–Fri 3,000 Ft., Sat/Sun 3,400 Ft., children 2,300/2,500 Ft. | XIII | Margaret Island | www.palatinusstrand. hu | bus 26, 226*

TROPICARIUM ● (138 C6) (*ø 0*)

The chief attraction of this underwater world are sharks that swim past the visitors in a tunnel. Apart from huge aquariums with many plants and animals, there is also a rainforest with birds and reptiles. *Daily 10am–8pm | XXII | Nagytétényi út 37–45 | in the Campona shopping centre | admission 2,500 Ft., children 1,800 Ft. | www.tropicarium.hu | bus 33 Lépcsős utca (from metro station Móricz Zsigmond körtér, approx. 25 minutes)*

FESTIVALS & EVENTS

FESTIVALS & EVENTS

JANUARY

New Year's Day concerts are tradition-ally held in the St. Stephen's Basilica on 1 January *(www.organconcert.hu)* on its majestically sounding organ, which is protected as a listed instrument. Church music concerts take place on January 2 with works from Bach Vivaldi and Liszt. A contemplative start to the New Year!

MARCH

★ **Budapest Spring Festival** *(www.btf. hu)* with events and concerts from clas-sical to jazz and folk. This is Hungary's largest art festival, involving the national artist elite as well as international stars of the cultural scene. Usually takes place during the second half of the month.

MAY

Majális: Fun celebrations all over the city on May 1 to mark Labour Day. Rather than organising demos, Budapest locals go for picnics, visit open-air concerts and other events, e.g. in the municipal forest. The annual INSIDER TIP **International co-mic festival** is held every year in *Dürer Kert* (see p. 81) in early/mid May and at-tracts a friendly crowd of comic fans.

Jewish Art Days Festival *(www.jewish festival.hu):* A series of programs aimed at anyone interested in Jewish culture. Concerts, parties, discussions, theatre... and watch out for performances from ● *Budapest Klezmer Band* and *Budapest Bár*.

JUNE

In mid-June there is a week-long celebra-tion of the **Danube Carnival** *(www.duna karneval.hu)*. Much dance and folklore at various venues. It ends on Saturday with a large, colourful procession through the centre of Pest.

JULY

Budapest Pride *(www.budapestpride. hu):* Budapest has been out on the streets demonstrating for homosexual rights for over 20 years. Today, *Pride* is an enormous celebration for everyone who supports tolerance and an open-minded culture. A great event with an exciting program of performances and side acts.
Formula 1 – Hungarian Grand Prix *(www. hungaroring.hu):* The stars of interna-tional racing sport gather at the Hun-garoring to the east of Budapest every summer. Would you prefer to take to the wheel yourself? Then try the INSIDER TIP go-kart track in the centre of the ring!

AUGUST

The **Sziget Festival** *(www.szigetfestival.com)*: Held on the island Óbuda (Óbudai sziget), the festival takes place every year in early/mid August. It's worth going there at least once in your lifetime, if only for a day and become a *Szitizen*. A diverse spectrum of music is played to a very international crowd of revellers.

On 20 August for the national holiday commemorating Hungary's first king ★ **St Stephen's Day** Budapest holds a fireworks display on the Danube in the evening –with lots of pálinka (fruit brandies).

OCTOBER

Spar Budapest Marathon *(www.budapestmarathon.com)*: Autumn in Budapest is a time for marathons. A half marathon is already held in September.

International Harp Festival *(www.kiralykastely.hu)*: one of the best in the world, in the magnificent setting of Gödöllő Palace.

DECEMBER

The best Christmas lights can be found near and in Andrássy út, and in Vörösmarty tér there is also a **Christmas Market** selling arts and crafts.

On 30 December the **festival concert of the 100-strong Budapest Gypsy Symphony Orchestra** *(www.argosart.hu)* is held in the Convention Hall (can also be booked with dinner).

New Year's Eve: On 31 December half of Budapest is on the streets. Several places have stages offering ● free live music, and toy trompets cause happy noises.

NATIONAL HOLIDAYS

1 Jan	New Year's Day
15 March	Day of the Hungarian Revolution of 1848 (national holiday)
22 April 2019, 13 April 2020	Easter Monday
1 May	Labour Day
10 June 2019, 1 June 2020	Whit Monday
20 Aug	Day of St Stephen (national holiday)
23 Oct	Day of the Republic, commemorating the 1956 uprising (national holiday)
1 Nov	All Saints' Day
25/26 Dec	Christmas

LINKS, BLOGS, APPS & MORE

welovebudapest.com Stylish site with interactive map, tips for accomodation, cafés and restaurants, sightseeing, events and the latest trends in Budapest

underguide.com For those who want to explore Budapest in a more unusual style: Tailored, personal city tours with locals, bar hopping, group and business events such as a "ghoulash cooking contest"

www.funzine.hu Budapest's hip event and lifestyle magazine is available online (in English and Hungarian) as well in hard copy as a free handout to be picked up at entrances to restaurants, pubs and hostels

www.direkt36.hu/en *Direkt36* iis a non-profit project for investigative journalism (also in English) – with online in-depth reporting on corruption and allegations in Hungarian politics

www.budapestbylocals.com Extensive blog with lots of exciting tips for Budapest posted by a friendly Hungarian couple in English

est.hu A List of all English-language films showing in Budapest as well as different events such as concerts and exhibitions etc.

en.budapestgaycity.net/events Most LGBTQ+ events are listed here and at *www. qalendar.hu.* Another interesting site is *www.humenonline.hu,* the first gay magazine in Hungary – online but also available as a free handout

runinbudapest.com Budapest likes to call itself "the new running capital of Europe", and there are indeed no less than five marathon events during the year. Here you can find information on all of them

www.facebook.com/pusztastranger Political and contemporary blog about

the latest developments in Hungary and Budapest especially. Here you can find critical views and often uncomfortable information which are not disclosed to tourists

www.spottedbylocals.com/budapest Locals offer advice on what's in, where to go and the latest shopping destinations and exhibitions in and around Budapest (in English)

www.facebook.com/ablakamultra Take a look through a "Window to the past": the photographer Zoltán Kerényi uses old black and white photos and inserts them into photos of Hungary today – the result is amazing. You can spend hours scrolling through the photos. Particularly well presented at *www.flickr.com/photos/mrsultan/sets/72157626149118210*

www.budapestinfo.hu The official website of the Budapest tourism office is well designed and provides lots of information on the Budapest Card, events and opening times

www.youtube.com/user/BalconyTVBudapest Listen to some of the young Hungarian music bands around and watch live performances of international acts – all filmed from a balcony in Budapest. This innovative project has now ended yet the videos are well made and worth watching

www.youtube.com/user/szigetofficial/videos This official channel of the Sziget music festival contains funny and inspiring videos about music and the city

www.budapest.com/stadtfuhrer/multimedia/video.de.html Tour of the city in six and half minutes – the video "Budapest Thank You is Köszönöm" for young people shows popular nightlife haunts and important places to see (in English)

VIDEOS & MUSIC

MAPS.ME Offline maps and navi function – simply download the map you need. Interesting points of attraction are also displayed on the map – a very helpful app

Budapest Design Map An English-language app designed especially for the Budapest Design Week with great tips and advice on design hotspots. A must-have for fashionistas!

APPS

TRAVEL TIPS

ARRIVAL

Hungarian motorways are toll roads. Vignettes *(matrica)* are available for purchase at the border and at service stations. They cost 2,975 Ft. for ten days and 4,780 Ft. for 31 days. Keep your receipt *(www.autobahn.hu)*. From the north and west you can reach Budapest via highway M1. It is no fun to be travelling in the city with a car, not least because of the lack of parking spaces. It is advisable to leave your vehicle in the hotel garage or on a guarded parking lot.

Train connections have got better and faster. The train journey from London to Budapest takes just 24 hours, by Eurostar to Paris and high-speed TGV from Paris to Munich, then railjet train (approx. 7 hours). Or there are connections via Brussels, Cologne & Vienna. All long-distance trains arrive in Budapest at the Eastern Station (Keleti pályaudvar) (132 C5) *(ⓜ G9)* , trains from Vienna also stop at Kelenföld (139 D5) *(ⓜ O)*. *Train information: www.seat61.com | www. mav.hu. International train information Budapest: tel. 1 4 44 44 99*

There are coach connections with many cities in western Europe *(www. eurolines.com)*. The international bus station is *Népliget (IX | Üllői utca 131 | metro 3: Népliget)* (137 E5) *(ⓜ J13)*.

The standard national airlines such as British Airways and Malév offer several Budapest flight a day. Among the cheaper airlines, there are flights from London and Manchester with *Easyjet (www.easyjet.com)* and *Jet2 (www.jet2. com),* as well as from most western European cities. American Airlines operate direct flights from New York.
Situated on the southeast city fringes is the *Liszt Ferenc International Airport* with terminals 2A and 2B.
An inexpensive way to get into the city is to take the express bus 200E to the last stop on underground line 3, Kőbánya-Kispest. From there head to the city centre. The best way is to buy a multi-day ticket or the *Budapest Card* (from the *BudapestInfo Pont)* which entitles you to free use of public transport. Or use the airport shuttle mini buses *(tel. 1 2 96 85 55 | www.airportshuttle.hu)* that will drive you to any address in Budapest (one way ticket first person 3,200 Ft.). A taxi into the city will cost between 6,500 and 7,000 Ft, depending on your destination zone.

RESPONSIBLE TRAVEL

While traveling you can influence a lot. Don't just keep track of your carbon footprint *(www.myclimate.org)* by planning an ecologically harmless route. Also think about how you can protect nature and culture abroad *(www.ecotrans.org)*. It is all the more important that as a tourist you take into consideration aspects such as the conservation of nature *(www. wwf.org)*, regional products, minimal use of cars, saving water and many more things. For more information on ecological Tourism look at *www. ecotourism.org*.

From June to the end of September hydrofoils operate three times a week on the Danube between Vienna and Budapest (journey time 5 ½ hrs., one-way ticket approx. 30,700 Ft.). *www.mahart passnave.hu*

CITY TOURS

You can book city tours *(városnézés)* during the day or at night, tours of the Hungarian Parliament Building and trips to Buda Castle in hotels, travel agencies and tourist offices. City tours, some in open buses, are run e.g. by *Giraffe Hop-on-Hop-off (tel. 1 3 74 70 75 | www.citytour. hu)*. There are 43 different stops on three lines where you can get on and off as the mood takes you. A boat trip and a tour on foot are also included. Another operator is *Programcentrum (tel. 1 3 17 77 67 | www. programcentrum.hu)*. You can explore Budapest by day and by night with *Absolute Walking Tours (www.absolutetours.com)*. Another option is a Segway Tour (duration 2–hrs.). *Discover Budapest Tour Center (VI | Lázár utca 16 | behind the opera | tel. 1 2 69 33 43 | www.discoverbudapest.com)* Boat trips: *Duna Bella/Dunai Legenda (tel. 1 2 66 41 90 | www.legenda.hu)*. You can also join Danube trips such as *Budapest by Night* and trips to the Danube Bend (pier Vigadó tér) *(www.mahart passnave.hu)*.

CONSULATES & EMBASSIES

UK EMBASSY
Füge utca 5–7 | 1022 Budapest | tel. 1 2 66 28 88| www.gov.uk/government/ world/hungary

US EMBASSY
Szabadság tér 12 | 1054 Budapest | tel. 1 4 75 44 00| hu.usembassy.gov

BUDGETING

Cappuccino	£ 1.22/$ 1.72 per cup
Lunch menu	approx. £ 2.60–6.97/$ 3.68–9.80 for a lunch menu in a restaurant
Beer	£ 1.22/$ 1.72 per glass (0.5 l)
Taxi	£ 0.78/$ 1.10 per kilometre
Metro	£ 1,22/$ 1,72 for a 72-hour ticket encompassing the regional network
Thermal baths	£ 11/$ 16 for a day ticket, incl. changing cubicle

CUSTOMS

Goods for personal consumption can be imported and exported for free within the EU, e.g. 10 l spirits, 90 l wine or 800 cigarettes per person. Non-commercial quantities of items purchased or received are not subject to custom duties in Hungary but may be subject to the custom duties and import regulations of a destination country outside the EU.

CYCLING

You are faster and more flexible travelling by bike than you are with public transport.

The city's government is doing what it can – albeit slowly – to extend the network of bike paths. You may also spot the bright green city bikes: to use one of these so-called *BuBi (molbubi.bkk.hu)*, you need to register at one of the 100 docking stations around the city or at the counters of the Budapest transport operator (BKK). The easiest way to hire a bike is by smartphone or using your credit card. Once you hire a *BuBi*, the first 30 minutes are for free! Cycle tours are run by *Yellow Zebra Bike Tours (VI | Lázár utca 16 | www. yellowzebrabikes.com)*. Yellow Zebra also rents out bikes, so you can set off on your own. Guided bike tours and bike hire are also offered by *HiBike (Apáczai Csere János utca 3 | www.hibikebudapest.com)*.

DRIVING

The maximum speed in Hungary in towns and cities is 50kph, outside towns and cities it is 90kph and on motorways 130kph. Outside towns you must have dipped headlights on during the day too. There is a zero-tolerance policy when it comes to drinking and a seatbelt must be worn on every seat. Talking on mobile phones is only permitted with a hands-free set. You must carry high-visibility jackets (one for every seat in the vehicle). In the event of a crash where people were injured, the police must be notified. Take your green insurance card.
– Breakdown and emergency service of the Hungarian automobile club (*Magyar Autóklub MAK, Yellow Angels/Sárga angyal): tel. 188*
– International emergency number: tel. 1 3 45 17 44

EMERGENCY

Ambulance: *tel. 104* (emergency ambulance free, if an immediate medical in-

tervention is necessary); Police: *tel. 107,* hotline: *tel. 1 4 38 80 80;* Fire: *tel. 105*

IMMIGRATION

All you need to enter Hungary is a passport. US citizens may enter Hungary for up to 90 days for tourist or business purposes without a visa.

INFORMATION BEFORE YOU GO

HUNGARIAN NATIONAL TOURIST OFFICE
– *46 Eaton Place | London SW1X8AL | tel. 020 78 23 10 55 | gotohungary.com*
– *223 East 52nd Street | New York | NY 10022 | tel. 212 695 1221 | www.gotohungary.com*

You will find information also on *www.budapestinfo.hu* or *www.budapest.com*.

INFORMATION IN BUDAPEST

BUDAPEST FESTIVAL AND TOURIST CENTRE
– *V | Deák Ferenc tér/Sütő utca 2 | tel. 1 4 38 80 80 | metro 1, 2, 3: Deák Ferenc tér* (125 D2) *(ØØ D9)*
– *VI | Liszt Ferenc tér 11 | metro 1: Oktogon* (131 F4) *(ØØ E8)*
– *airport Liszt Ferenc: Terminal 2A and 2B | bus 200E* (0) *(ØØ 0)*
– *www.budapestinfo.hu*

INTERNET ACCESS

The density of WiFi hotspots is generally high. There is free WiFi in almost all cafés, restaurants and pubs in the inner city as well as in shopping centres (e.g. Westend in Pest, Mammut in Buda), in the coffeehouse chains and at the airport.

MEDIA

International daily newspapers are available especially at *Inmedio* newsagents (red sign, e.g. at *Városház utca 3–5)*, from kiosks in the touristy areas in the city centre (Vörösmarty tér, Váci utca) and in large hotels. The Budapest Times *(www.budapesttimes.hu)* is Hungary's leading English-language source for daily news, restaurants, hotels, movies, culture and tourism. The satellite channels are accessible everywhere.

MONEY & BANKS

The currency in Hungary is the forint (Ft., HUF). Changing money is possible in banks, travel agencies, bureaux de change and through money-changing machines (in banks). Be careful with the bureaux de change at the airport and in the city centre as the exchange rate is often very unfavorable. Banks are usually open Mon–Thu 8am–4pm and Fri 8am–3pm. You will also be able to get money with the usual credit/debit cards (banks, ATMs). And you can pay with your credit card almost everywhere (supermarkets, restaurants, pubs, taxis).

OPENING HOURS & ADMISSION PRICES

Specialist shops are usually open Mon-Fri from 10am to 6pm and on Saturdays between 10am and 1pm. Shopping centres (sometimes open on Sundays) and supermarkets often have longer opening times. Museums are usually open Tue–Sun from 10am to 6pm, yet often close earlier in winter at 4pm. Admission prices generally are (still) below the western European standards – priced between around 3 and 6 euros. Museums which attract lots of tourists usually ask for more which is unfortunately not always reflected in the quality of the exhibitions. If prices are written in euros, you should especially consider whether you really want to visit the museum or not.

PHONE & MOBILE PHONE

Phone numbers in Budapest have seven digits, the city dialling code is 1. For a local call from a landline you can omit the 1. From a landline in Hungary (long distance) as well as from Hungarian mobile phones you have to dial 06 as well as the area code, i.e. for Budapest

CURRENCY CONVERTER

£	HUF	HUF	£
1	364	10	0.03
3	1,092	50	0.14
5	1,820	250	0.69
13	4,733	750	2.06
40	14,563	2,000	5,49
75	27,305	5,000	13.73
120	43,689	12,000	32,96
250	91,000	30,000	82
500	182,000	50,000	137

$	HUF	HUF	$
1	272	10	0.035
3	816	50	0.18
5	1,360	250	0.92
13	3,536	750	2.76
40	10,880	2,000	7.35
75	20,400	5,000	18
120	32,644	12,000	44
250	68,000	30,000	110
500	136,000	50,000	183

For current exchange rates see www.xe.com

061, followed by the phone number. The country dialling code for Hungary is 0036; if you want to call a Budapest number from a landline outside of Hungary, you have to dial 00361, then the phone number. Hungarian mobile phone numbers also have seven digits and usually start with 20, 30 or 70. To call one, from a Hungarian landline or mobile, you always have to prefix it by 06 (e.g. 0620, then the seven-digit number). To call the UK, dial 0044, to call the USA, dial 001, then the local area code minus the 0 and then the phone number.

POST

Post offices are generally open Mon–Fri 8am–6pm and Sat 8am–noon. The postage for standard letters and postcards to European countries is 335 Ft.

PUBLIC TRANSPORT

The nicest underground line, opened in 1896, is *Földalatti* (Line 1). There are three further underground lines (metro) – the red line 2, the blue line 3 and the green line 4 – as well as a dense network of trams, buses and trolley-buses. To get up to Castle Hill you can take the funicular *(Sikló)*, which departs from Clark Ádám tér and needs an extra ticket.

There are commuter lines *(HÉV)* running along the northern right bank of the Danube (towards the Danube Bend) and along the southern left bank, as well as (in the east) towards Gödöllő. You can take a cog railway *(Fogaskerekűvasút)* into the hills around Budapest: it departs from Városmajor on the Buda side; you can also take this railway to get to the Children's Railway *(Gyermekvasút)*.

Tickets can in most cases only be purchased before you get on the train (met-

WEATHER IN BUDAPEST

	Jan	Feb	March	April	May	June	July	Aug	Sept	Oct	Nov	Dec
Daytime temperatures in °C/°F	2/36	4/40	11/52	17/63	22/72	26/79	28/82	27/81	23/73	16/61	8/46	3/37
Nighttime temperatures in °C/°F	−3/27	−2/28	2/36	6/43	11/52	14/57	16/61	15/59	12/54	7/45	3/37	−1/30
☀	2	3	4	6	8	8	9	9	7	5	2	1
☂	8	7	7	7	9	8	7	6	6	8	9	9

TRAVEL TIPS

ro stations, machines); the metro stations are your best option because you can get every kind of ticket there. You will have to cancel your ticket in a machine in the train, or in the underground in machines by the escalators and on the platforms. Timed tickets are usually stamped with the exact times pan in which they are valid. You must hold on to your ticket until you have left the station, because the inspectors usually stand at the exits. A single ticket (350 Ft.) is valid for the whole line, but if you switch lines, you must purchase a new ticket. It is cheaper and simpler to buy a ticket for 24 or 72 hours or a weekly ticket (1,650/4,150/4,950 Ft., valid for all means of public transport in Budapest). Liners run regularly between the Rákóczi bridge in the south, downtown and Újpest in the north (lines D11, 12), in summer also on weekends to Margaret Island and to Óbuda (Line D13).
Timetables and further information on traffic: *BKK (VII | Rumbach Sebestyén utca 19–21/corner of Király utca | tel. 1 3 25 52 55 | www.bkk.hu).*

REDUCTIONS

EU citizens who are pensioners (aged 65 and older) can use Hungary's public transport (buses, trains) for free. If you are checked, you must show identification. School pupils and students from the EU and Switzerland are given a 50 percent discount at the Budapest Public Transport Company BKK (get your ID cards ready!). The *Budapest Card* (available e.g. at airports and at the Budapest Tourist Office) gives you unlimited use of public transport and offers a wealth of further advantages and reductions. It costs 5,500 Ft. (24 hrs), 8,500 Ft. (48 hrs) or 10,900 Ft. (72 hrs). *More info and online order: www.budapestinfo.hu*

TAXIS

The taxi rates are set prices: the basic fee is 450 Ft., 280 Ft. per kilometre plus 70 Ft. per waiting minute. All taxis must be officially painted in the same shade of yellow and have a license sticker on the side. As there are still some black sheep driving around, you should really phone up to book a taxi: *Green Taxi (electric cars only): tel. 1 4 00 00 00 | City Taxi: tel. 1 2 11 11 11*

TICKET SALES

Ticket Express (131 E5) *(D–E 8–9)
(Mon–Fri 10am–6pm | VI | Dálszínház utca 10 | tel. 30 3 03 09 99 | www. eventim.hu | metro 1: Opera)*

TIME

Budapest, like all of Hungary, uses Central European Time (CET) and Central European Summer Time (CEST).

TIPPING & SERVICE FEES

A tip of 10 percent is customary in restaurants and pubs, but it's not expected when you order at the bar. Restaurants (but not snack bars) are allowed to raise a service charge of up to 15 per cent which will be shown on the check. That's not the rule, but it never hurts to be vigilant if you don't want to pay double tips in the end.

WHEN TO GO

Spring and autumn are the best times to go to Budapest. During the summer months the city is often extremely crowded and gets very hot.

USEFUL PHRASES HUNGARIAN

PRONUNCIATION

To help you say the words, we have added a simplified pronunciation guide (in square brackets). The stress is always on the first syllable of a word. Please note also:

ö   is pronounced like the "e" in "the"
ü   is pronounced like the "u" in French "tu"
gy   is pronounced like "dy" in "dew"
g   is pronounced as in "go"

IN BRIEF

Yes/No/Maybe	Igen [igen]/Nem [nem]/Talán [tollaan]
Please/Thank you	Kérem [kayrem]/Köszönöm [kössönöm]
Excuse me, please!	Bocsáss meg! [botchaash meg]/Bocsásson meg, kérem! [botchaashonn meg, kayrem]
May I...?/Pardon?	Szabad...? [sobbodd]/Tessék? [teshshayk]
I would like to.../ Have you got...?	Szeretnék [seretnayk]/ Van...? [vonn]
How much is...?	Mennyibe kerül? [mennyiber kerül]
I (don't) like that	Ez (nem) tetszik [ez (nem) tetsik]
good/bad	jó [yo]/rossz [ross]
broken/doesn't work	rossz [ross]/nem működik [nem müköddikk]
too much/much/little	túl sok [tool shokk]/sok [shokk]/kevés [kevaysh]
all/nothing	minden [minden]/semmi [shemmi]
Help!/Attention!/ Caution!	Segítség! [shegichayg]/Figyelem! [fidyelem]/Vigyázat! [vidyaazott]
ambulance/police/ fire brigade	mentő [menter]/rendőrség [rendershayg]/ tűzoltóság [tüzoltoshaag]
Prohibition/forbidden	tilalom [tilollom]/tilos [tillosh]
danger/dangerous	veszély [vessay]/veszélyes [vessayesh]
May I take a photo here/ of you?	Szabad itt/Önt fényképezni? [sobod eet/önt faynye-kaypessni]

GREETINGS, FAREWELL

Good morning!/afternoon!/ evening!/night!	Jó reggelt/[yo reggelt]/napot! [yo noppot]/ estét [yo eshtayt]/éjszakát! [yo ayssokkaat]
Hello!/Goodbye!	Halló! [hallo]/Viszontlátásra! [vissontlaataashro]

Beszélsz Magyarul?

"Do you speak Hungarian?" This guide will help you to say the basic words and phrases in Hungarian.

See you	Szia/Sziasztok! [sio/siosstok]
My name is...	...-nak hívnak [...-nokk heefnokk]
What's your name?	Hogy hívják Önt? [hody heefyaak önt]/ Hogy hívnak? [hody heefnokk]

DATE & TIME

Monday/Tuesday/	hétfő [haytföö]/kedd [ked]
Wednesday/Thursday	szerda [sairdo]/csütörtök [chüttörrtökk]
Friday/Saturday	péntek [payntek]/szombat [sombott]
Sunday/working day	vasárnap [voshaarnopp]/munkanap [munkonopp]
holiday	ünnepnap [ünnepnopp]
today/tomorrow/yesterday	ma [mo]/holnap [holnopp]/tegnap [tegnopp]
hour/minute/day/night	óra [oaro]/perc [pairts]/nap [nopp]/éjszaka [ayssokko]
What time is it?	Hány óra (van)? [haany oaro (vonn)]
It's three o'clock	Három óra (van) [haarom oaro (vonn)]
It's half past three	Fél négy (van) [fayl naydy (vonn)]
a quarter to four/	Háromnegyed négy (van) [haaromnedyed naydy
a quarter past four	(vonn)]/Negyed öt (van) [nedyed ött (vonn)]

TRAVEL

open/closed	nyitva [nyitvo]/zárva [zaarvo]
entrance/exit	bejárat [bayaarotl]/kijárat [kiyaarott]
departure/arrival	indulás [indulaash]/érkezés [ayrkezaysh]
toilets/ladies/gentlemen	toalett [toallet]/hölgyek [höldyekk]/urak [urrokk]
(no) drinking water	(nem) ívóvíz [(nem) eevoveez]
Where is...?/Where are...?	Hol van ...? [hol vonn]/Hol vannak ...? [hol vonnokk]
left/right	balra [bollro]/jobbra [yobro]
straight ahead/back	egyenes(en) [edyenesh(en)]/vissza [visso]
close/far	közel [kerzel]/messze [messer]
bus/tram / taxi/cab	busz [buss]/villamos [vilommosh] / taxi [toxi]
U-Bahn/bus stop	metró [metro]/megálló [megalo]
parking lot/parking garage	parkoló [porrkolo]/parkolóház [porrkolohaaz]
street map/map	várostérkép [vaaroshtayrkayp]/térkép [tayrkayp]
train station	vasútállomás [voshootaalomaash]
airport	repülőtér [repülertayr]
schedule/ticket	menetrend [menetrend]/menetjegy [menetyedy]
single/return	oda [odo]/oda-vissza [odo-vissa]
train/track	vonat [vonott]/vágány [vaagaany]
I would like to rent...	...-t szeretnék bérelni [seretnayk bayrelni]
a car/a bicycle	autót [owto]/biciklit [bitsiklit]

petrol/gas station	benzinkút [benzeenkoot]
petrol/gas / diesel	benzin [benzeen]/gázolaj [gaazoloy]
breakdown/repair shop	defekt [defekt]/műhely [mühay]

FOOD & DRINK

Could you please book a table for tonight for four?	Foglaljon kérem nekünk ma estére egy asztalt négy személyre [foglalyon kayrem nekünk mo eshtayrer edy osstollt naydy semayrer]
The menu, please	Az étlapot kérem [os aytlopot kayrem]
Could I please have...?	Hozna nekem kérem...? [hosno nekem kayrem]
salt/pepper/sugar/vinegar	só [sho]/bors [borsh]/cukor [tsukor]/ecet [etset]
milk/cream/lemon/oil	tej [tay]/tejszín [tayseen]/citrom [tsitrom]/olaj [oloy]
with/without ice/ sparkling	jéggel [yaygel]/jég nélkül [yayg naykül]/szénsavas [saynshovosh]/szénsavmentes [saynnshan-mentesh]
vegetarian/allergy	vegetáriánus [vegetaariaanush]/allergia [olairgio]
May I have the bill, please?	Fizetni szeretnék, kérem [fizzetni seretnayk, kayrem]
bill/receipt	számla [saamlo]/nyugta [nyoogto]

SHOPPING

I'd like.../I'm looking for...	Szeretnék... [seretnayk]/Keresek ... [keresek]
pharmacy/chemist	gyógyszertár [dyodyssairtaar]/drogéria [drogayrio]
baker/market/kiosk	pékség [paykshayg]/piac [piots]/trafik [trofik]
100 grammes/1 kilo	száz gramm [saas grom]/egy kiló [edy kilo]
expensive/cheap/price	drága [draago]/olcsó [olcho]/ár [aar]
more/less	több [töb]/kevesebb [kevvesheb]

ACCOMMODATION

I have booked a room	Szobát rendeltem [sobaat rendeltem]
Do you have any... left?	Van még szabad...? [vonn mayg sobod]
single room	egyágyas szobájuk [eddyaadyosh sobaayukk]
double room	kétágyas szobájuk [kaytaadyosh sobaayukk]
breakfast/half board	reggeli [reggeli]/félpanzió [faylponsioan]
full board (American plan)/ Balkon	teljes panzió [telyesh ponsioan]/ erkély [airkay]
shower/sit-down bath	tusoló [toosholo]/fürdőszoba [fürdösobo]
key/room card	kulcs [kultch]/szobakártya [sobokaartyo]
luggage/suitcase	csomag [chomogg]/bőrönd [börönnd]

BANKS, MONEY & CREDIT CARDS

bank/ATM	bank [bonk]/bankautomata [bonkowtomaato]
pin code	titkos kód [titkosh koad]
I'd like to change...	Szeretnék... váltani [seretnayk ... vaaltoni]

cash/credit card	készpénz [kayspaynz]/hitelkártya [hitelkartyo]
bill/coin	bankjegy [bonkyedy]/fémpénz [faympaynz]
change	aprópénz [opropaynz]

HEALTH

doctor/dentist/	orvos [orvosh]/fogorvos [fogorvos]/
paediatrician	gyerekorvos [dyerekorvos]
hospital/	kórház [koarhaas]/
emergency clinic	sürgősségi rendelés [shürgöshshaygi rendelaysh]
fever/pain	láz [laaz]/fájdalom [foydollom]
diarrhoea/nausea	hasmenés [hosmanaysh]/rosszullét [rossulayt]
pain reliever/	fájdalomcsillapító [foydollomchilopeeto]/
tablet	tabletta [tobletto]

POST, TELECOMMUNICATIONS & MEDIA

stamp/letter/postcard	bélyeg [bayeg]/levél [levayl]/képeslap [kaypeshlopp]
I need a landline phone card	Szükségem van telefonkártyára vezetékes telefonhoz [sükshaygem vonn telefonkartyaaro vesetaykesh telefonhoz]
I'm looking for a prepaid card for my mobile	Feltöltős telefonkártyát keresek a mobil-telefonomhoz [feltöltösh telefonkartyaat keresek o mobiltelefonomhoz]
internet access	internethozzáférés [internethossaafayraysh]

NUMBERS

0	nulla [nullo]	18	tizennyolc [tizzennyolts]
1	egy [edy]	19	tizenkilenc [tizzenkilents]
2	kettő/két [kettö/kayt]	20	húsz [hooss]
3	három [haarom]	21	huszonegy [hussonedy]
4	négy [naydy]	30	harminc [horrmints]
5	öt [öt]	40	negyven [nedyven]
6	hat [hott]	50	ötven [ötven]
7	hét [hayt]	60	hatvan [hottvonn]
8	nyolc [nyolts]	70	hetven [hetven]
9	kilenc [kilents]	80	nyolcvan [nyoltsvonn]
10	tíz [teess]	90	kilencven [kilentsven]
11	tizenegy [tizzenedy]	100	száz [saas]
12	tizenkettő/tizzenkét [tizenketter/tizzenkayt]	200	kétszáz [kaytsaas]
13	tizenhárom [tizzenhaarom]	1000	ezer [ezzer]
14	tizennégy [tizzennaydy]	2000	kétezer [kaytezzer]
15	tizenöt [tizzenöt]	10000	tízezer [teezzezzer]
16	tizenhat [tizzenhott]	½	fél [fayl]
17	tizenhét [tizzenhayt]	¼	(egy) negyed [(edy) nedyed]

STREET ATLAS

The green line indicates the Discovery Tour "Budapest at a glance"
The blue line indicates the other Discovery Tours
All tours are also marked on the pull-out map

Photo: Museum of Applied Arts

Exploring Budapest

The map on the back cover shows how the area has been sub-divided

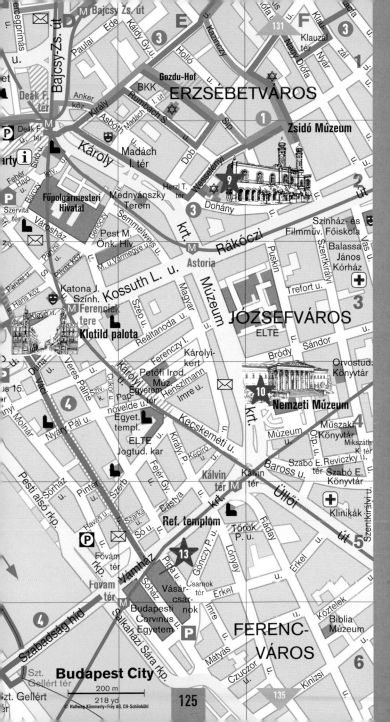

u.

D

E Országház

131

F

Néprajzi Múzeum

Kossuth Lajos tér

1

M HÉV **Batthyány tér**

4

Lajos

Szt. Anna templom

Batthyány tér

Szt. Anna
templom

Mark.

Aranyhal

1

5

II. Rákóczi Ferenc

Vértanuk tére

4

M

VÍZI-

VÁROS

Vám

Fő u.

Batthyány tér

Antall

Kossuth Lajos tér

Garibaldi

Nádor

u.

2

Vám

Székely

Szilágyi D.

4

Kossuth Lajos tér

Zoltán

Akadémia

u.

Toldi

tér

Gábor

Cipők a Duna-parton

József

Zoltán

Steindl Imre

u.

Donáti

Corvin tér

u.

Halász

Bem

Széchenyi

Széchenyi

u.

emplom

1

Halászbástya

Halász

Ponty u.

Kapucinus u.

rakpart

Magyar Tudományos Akadémia

4

Arany János u.

Tükory u.

u.

Hunyadi János

Szalag

Pala

Jégverem

4

3

Vigyázó F.u.

Ponty u.

Csónak u.

Szalag

Apor P.u.

rakpart

Széchenyi

Széchenyi István

Zrínyi u.

Hunyadi János

u.

Szt. Király

1

Széchenyi lánchíd

P

István

Mérleg

Dísz tér

Jane Haining

1

Várszínház
Nem. Tancszín.

4

Deák Ferenc tér

BELVÁROS

P

Sándor palota

Clark Ádám tér

Eötvös tér

1

Szt. György u.

Magyar
Nemz. Gal.

P

Friedrich

Várkert

Born

4

Apáczai Csere J. u.

Dunakorzó

Duna

2

Lovarda u.

3

1

Lánchíd

Ortnáz u.

rakpart

Vigadó tér

4

Budavári palota

Dunakorzó

Sarló u.

zsa Gy. tér

Dozsa György

Széchényi Könyvtár

Tört. Múz.

Ybl Miklós tér

4

P

Ybl Miklós tér

Várkert bazár

Buda Vár

Varalja

Krisztina

Attila

Várkert Bazár
Orvostörténeti
Múzeum

Atatürk

rakpart

rakpart

200 m

218 yd

© Hallwag Kümmerly+Frey AG, CH-Schönbühl

6

Pásztor u.

Szarvas tér

Krt.

Út

Döbrentei u.

Apród u.

Fogas

Fátyol

TABÁN

127

124

Tabáni templom

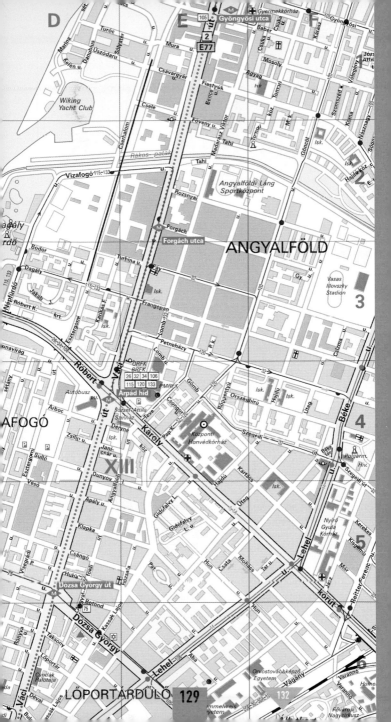

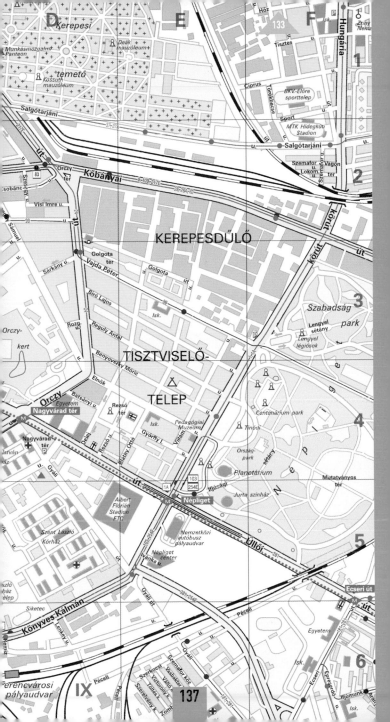

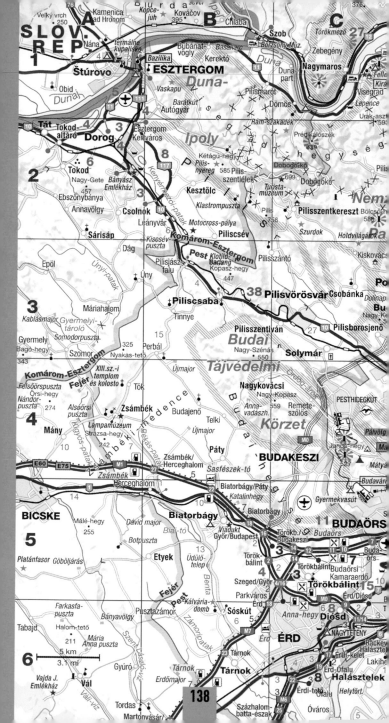

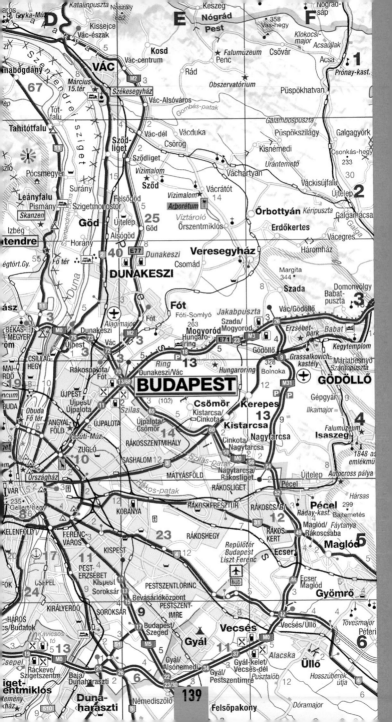

This index contains a selection of the streets and squares shown on the street atlas

KEY TO STREET ATLAS

Autópálya / Autobahn		Motorway / Autoroute
Négysávos út / Vierspurige Straße		Road with four lanes / Route à quatre voies
Átmenő út / Durchgangsstraße		Thoroughfare / Route de transit
Főútvonal / Hauptstraße		Main road / Route principale
Egyéb út / Sonstige Straßen		Other roads / Autres routes
Információ - Parkolóhely / Information - Parkplatz	ℹ 🅿	Information - Parking place / Information - Parking
Hajókikötő - Hajóútvonal / Anlegestelle - Schifffahrtslinie	⚓	Landing place - Shipping route / Embarcadère - Ligne de navigation
Egyirányú utca - Sétálóutca / Einbahnstraße - Fußgängerzone		One-way street - Pedestrian zone / Rue à sens unique - Zone piétonne
Fővasútvonal állomással / Hauptbahn mit Bahnhof		Main railway with station / Chemin de fer principal avec gare
Egyéb vasútvonal / Sonstige Bahn		Other railway / Autre ligne
Kötélpálya / Standseilbahn		Cableway / Funiculaire
Földalatti vasút / U-Bahn	M	Underground / Métro
Villamos - Gyorsjárat / Straßenbahn - Schnellbuslinie	4 13	Tramway - Express bus-route / Tramway - Ligne d'autobus à service rapide
Autóbuszvonal - Trolibuszvonal / Buslinie - O-Buslinie	24 75	Bus-route - Trolleybus-route / Ligne d'autobus - Ligne de trolleybus
Templom - Látványos templom / Kirche - Sehenswerte Kirche		Church - Church of interest / Église - Église remarquable
Zsinagóga - Kápolna / Synagoge - Kapelle		Synagogue - Chapel / Synagogue - Chapelle
Postahivatal / Postamt	✆	Post office / Bureau de poste
Rendőrség - Emlékmű / Polizeistation - Denkmal	● ♈	Police station - Monument / Poste de police - Monument
Kórház - Ifjúsági szálló / Krankenhaus - Jugendherberge	⊕ ▲	Hospital - Youth hostel / Hôpital - Auberge de jeunesse
Beépítés - Középületek / Bebauung - Öffentliches Gebäude		Built-up area - Public building / Zone bâtie - Bâtiment public
Iparvidék - Park, erdő / Industriegelände - Park, Wald		Industrial area - Park, forest / Zone industrielle - Parc, bois
MARCO POLO 1. élménytúra / MARCO POLO Erlebnistour 1		MARCO POLO Discovery Tour 1 / MARCO POLO Tour d'aventure 1
MARCO POLO élménytúrák / MARCO POLO Erlebnistouren		MARCO POLO Discovery Tours / MARCO POLO Tours d'aventure
MARCO POLO Highlight	★	MARCO POLO Highlight

FOR YOUR NEXT TRIP...

MARCO POLO TRAVEL GUIDES

Travel with **Insider Tips**

INDEX

The index contains all of the attractions and museums in Budapest and all of the destinations described in this travel guide. Bold figures refer to the main entry.

CREDITS

WRITE TO US

e-mail: info@marcopologuides.co.uk

Did you have a great holiday?
Is there something on your mind?
Whatever it is, let us know!
Whether you want to praise, alert us
to errors or give us a personal tip –
MARCO POLO would be pleased to
hear from you.
We do everything we can to provide
the very latest information for your trip.

Nevertheless, despite all of our authors'
thorough research, errors can creep
in. MARCO POLO does not accept any
liability for this. Please contact us by
e-mail or post.

MARCO POLO Travel Publishing Ltd
Pinewood, Chineham Business Park
Crockford Lane, Chineham
Basingstoke, Hampshire RG24 8AL
United Kingdom

PICTURE CREDITS
Cover Photograph: Fisherman's Bastion (Corbis/Terra: S. Westmorland)
Photographs: Corbis/Terra: S. Westmorland (1); Fanni Király: Varga Gábor György (18 bottom); Getty Images: gehringj (12/13), J. Greuel (38), A. Hobel (5, 56/57), lechatnoir (108/109), D. Mohai (100), P. Ptschelinzew (50); Getty Images/AFP: A. Kisbenedek (107); huber-images: M. Borchi (30), R. Schmid (2, 4 bottom, 14, 58), R. Taylor (6, 37, 87), TC (9, 41, 70, 111), L. Vaccarella (26/27, 33, 90/91, 110 top); Laif: Barth (73), M. Galli (17, 79), E. Häberle (23, 62 right, 110 bottom), Hahn (95), H. Kloever (52), Modrow (63), D. Schmid (105), Stukhard (80), Zuder (84); Laif/roberth-arding: M. Runkel (11); Look: Fleisher (42), R. Mirau (flap left), I. Pompe (24, 88); Look/age fotostock (46); mauritius image/Trigger Image: N. Wright (19 bottom); mauritius images: D. Delimont (102), V. Preusser (68); mauritius images/Alamy: J. Beuge (62 left), M. G. Casella (55, 82/83), J. Kellerman (8), W. Lemlerkchai (20/21), Piya Travel (61), T. E. White (76); mauritius images/Blume Bild (34); mauritius images/Cultura (106); mauritius images/foodcollection: H. Krol (19 top); mauritius images/Image Source (74/75); mauritius images/imagebroker: M. Hauser (flap right, 106/107), P. Williams/Funkystock (122/123); mauritius images/Photononstop (4 top, 45, 100), mauritius images/Travel Collection: G. Hänel (7); mauritius images/Westend61 (3); picture-alliance/AP Photo: Z. Balogh (108); picture-alliance/dpa: A. Gebert (18 centre); picture-alliance/Shotshop: JB (10); A. Schlatterer (65); Trafó: Katalin Karsay (18 top); Visum: Heinze/Landmarker (48), S. Kiefer (66/67)

4th Edition – fully revised and updated 2019
Worldwide Distribution: Marco Polo Travel Publishing Ltd, Pinewood, Chineham Business Park, Crockford Lane, Basingstoke, Hampshire RG24 8AL, United Kingdom. Email: sales@marcopolouk.com
© MAIRDUMONT GmbH & Co. KG, Ostfildern
Chief editor: Marion Zorn
Author: Rita Stiens; Co-author: Matthias Eickhoff, Lisa Weil; Editor: Corinna Walkenhorst
Programme supervision: Lucas Forst-Gill, Susanne Heimburger, Johanna Jiranek, Nikolai Michaelis, Kristin Wittemann, Tim Wohlbold; Picture editors: Gabriele Forst, Anja Schlatterer; What's hot: wunder media, Munich
Cartography street atlas: © MAIRDUMONT, Ostfildern; Cartography pull-out map: © MAIRDUMONT, Ostfildern
Design front cover, p. 1, pull-out map cover: Karl Anders – Büro für Visual Stories, Hamburg; interior: milchhof:atelier, Berlin; Discovery Tours, p. 2/3: Susan Chaaban Dipl.-Des. (FH)
Translated from German by Susan Jones, Tübingen
Prepress: writehouse, Cologne; InterMedia, Ratingen
Phrase book in cooperation with Ernst Klett Sprachen GmbH, Stuttgart, Editorial by Pons Wörterbücher

MIX
Paper from responsible sources
FSC® C124385

DOS & DON'TS ☞

A few things you should avoid

DON'T FALL FOR FAKE POLICE OFFICERS

It doesn't happen often, but you could encounter someone posing as a police officer. Remember: police officers are allowed to check your papers on the street, but not your wallet!

DON'T LEAVE YOUR CAR UNGUARDED

Park your car for the duration of your stay on a safe car park with a surveillance system and never leave valuable objects or documents in it. New cars, especially German ones, are sought-after by car thieves. Book a space on a surveyed car park at *www.ezparkbuda pest.com* (select English language).

DON'T LOSE SIGHT OF YOUR VALUABLES

A favourite trick by pick-pockets is to take bags when they are hanging over the back of a chair. A safer option is to place your bag between your legs and keep your mobile somewhere in sight at all times. The same applies when you're travelling by public transport in the evenings after enjoying a beer.

DON'T CONSUME DRUGS

Keep your hands away from marihuana, ecstasy and other illegal drugs. Firstly, party drugs are often substituted for designer drugs which make their effect extremely unpredictable. Secondly, Hungary has strict laws on drugs: if you are caught in possession, you can face up to two years in prison.

DON'T ORDER WITHOUT CHECKING PRICES FIRST

In the past, Budapest restaurants and bars in tourist areas (e.g. in the Váci utca) were unfortunately notorious for charging extortionate prices on lunch and dinner bills. Always check the bill and ask when bread is brought to the table whether it's for free, for example.

DON'T MAKE BUSINESS ON THE STREET

Never change money on the street – that's illegal. The danger of being scammed is very high and you will possibly be robbed when you whip out your wallet. Don't be tempted to buy items such as iPhones and perfume on the street: you could easily become a victim of fraud.

DO BE CAREFUL WHEN CHANGING MONEY

Avoid exchanging currency at the airport as the rate of exchange is usually poor. Always check in exchange bureaus that the exchange rate being advertised will be paid out for your amount of money. Customers are often lured in by attractive exchange rates, but it's often the case that these only apply to large sums of money (e.g., £ 1,000). The easiest and safest way to pay is by credit card which is accepted almost everywhere.